Praise for *Free to Succeed*

"*Free to Succeed* will not only inspire you to create your dream career in the new economy but it also delivers the 'how-tos' with a clear, practical seven-step process for overcoming your fears, hurdling obstacles, and having fun at the same time."

—Mark S. Albion, author of
Making a Life, Making a Living

"*Free to Succeed* is smart because it doesn't give answers but asks the right questions. As a free agent, your major question is not whether your work is your passion—that's a given—but what type of free agent are you, and how and where will you do your best work? This book provides a framework—the structure, strategies, and step-by-step methods—for negotiating the new economy. Reinhold exacts a toll from readers: return on investments is based upon honest self-appraisal. But the reward is sweet: getting closer to your dreams faster—not only for satisfying and successful work but for a better life."

—Barbara Harris, editor-in-chief,
Shape magazine

BARBARA B. REINHOLD, ED.D., directs the career development center at Smith College. Her other enterprises include a private practice of counseling and coaching, and consulting to corporations, small businesses, nonprofits, schools, colleges, and government groups. She is also the online career coach for Monster.com. She lives with her family in western Massachusetts.

"Reinhold invites all those characters inside us—the rebel, the free spirit, the imagineer, the gambler, the philosopher, and the desperado—to share the stuff dreams are made of. Reinhold is right again—success in the brave new world means accepting the role of the free agent."

—Hugh Burns, chairman of the board,
The Daedalus Group, Inc.

"In a world where the old definition of job security no longer applies, this book provides invaluable and realistic new options—a must-read for all ages, all professions!"

—Carolyn Leighton, chairwoman/founder,
WITI (Women in Technology International)

"*Free to Succeed* has everything you need in one book to change not only your career but your approach to living. Barbara Reinhold believes that everyone has a right to a fulfilling life, and the means within themselves of obtaining it. Her book is essential reading for anyone working in the 21st century."

—Eileen O'Reilly, vice president,
Monster.com

"Barbara Reinhold's *Free to Succeed* is an excellent tool for navigating the new world of free agency. If you're ready to take the leap to self-employment, grab this book before you jump!"

—Terri Lonier, author of *Working Solo* and founder of SOHO Summit

" 'How do I win—or even survive—when the goal posts are moving continually?' 'How do I maintain equanimity in an environment of instability?' With more than one third of all American workers now free agents, Barbara Reinhold offers us this road map, enabling us to prosper and flourish in today's world of corporate and institutional upheaval and betrayal. She is a tough and realistic guide."

—Thomas A. Faulhaber, editor, The Business Forum Online®

"Getting the life you want is a lot like climbing Everest. And Barbara Reinhold is the Sherpa guide you want if you intend to take on the challenge. Enjoy this book—it will help you get where you want to go!"

—Joline Godfrey, author of *Twenty $ecrets to Independence: The DollarDiva's Guide to Life*

FREE to SUCCEED

Designing the Life You Want in the New Free Agent Economy

Barbara B. Reinhold, Ed.D.

A PLUME BOOK

*For the wonderful grown-up "kids" who so enrich my life,
Brooks, James, Geoffrey, and Greta,
in the hope that they'll always create for themselves
work lives filled with meaning, freedom, and fun.*

PLUME
Published by the Penguin Group
Penguin Putnam Inc., 375 Hudson Street, New York, New York 10014, U.S.A.
Penguin Books Ltd, 27 Wrights Lane, London W8 5TZ, England
Penguin Books Australia Ltd, Ringwood, Victoria, Australia
Penguin Books Canada Ltd, 10 Alcorn Avenue, Toronto, Ontario, Canada M4V 3B2
Penguin Books (N.Z.) Ltd, 182–190 Wairau Road, Auckland 10, New Zealand

Penguin Books Ltd, Registered Offices: Harmondsworth, Middlesex, England

First published by Plume, a member of Penguin Putnam Inc.

First Printing, May 2001

1 3 5 7 9 10 8 6 4 2

Illustration on page 59
by Wendy Simpson of Simpson and Green Graphics, Amherst, Massachusetts

Ⓟ REGISTERED TRADEMARK—MARCA REGISTRADA

LIBRARY OF CONGRESS CATALOGING-IN-PUBLICATION DATA:
Reinhold, Barbara Bailey.
Free to succeed : designing the life you want in the new free agent economy / by
Barbara B. Reinhold.
p.   cm.
ISBN 0-452-28251-9
1. Job satisfaction. 2. Work—Psychological aspects. I. Title.

HF5549.5.J63 R37 2001
650.14—dc21   00-049121

Printed in the United States of America

Set in Garamond Light

BOOKS ARE AVAILABLE AT QUANTITY DISCOUNTS WHEN USED TO PROMOTE PRODUCTS OR SERVICES.
FOR INFORMATION PLEASE WRITE TO PREMIUM MARKETING DIVISION, PENGUIN PUTNAM INC., 375
HUDSON STREET, NEW YORK, NEW YORK 10014.

ACKNOWLEDGMENTS

Many thanks, first of all, to the many people whose composite stories fill these pages. Without them there would be no book because I would know very little, outside of my own experiences and reading, about the peculiar thrills and stresses of free agency.

I'm also grateful to colleagues, friends, and family members who've given so generously of their time, hunting down resources, talking about these ideas at various stages in the process and reading drafts when their own lives were obviously crowded with obligations. Judy Allen, Bonnie Bailey Baker, Karen Blatt, Debbie Burke, Laurie Fenlason, Stephanie Fried, Lucy Greenburg, Barbara Harris, Carrie Hemenway, Bob Hill, Marilyn Huffman, Robin Kinder, Penny Locey, Donna Maimes, Judy McLamb, Paul Metevia, Joanne Murray, Deb Novak, Brooks Reinhold, Geoffrey Reinhold, Beth Rothenberg, Janice Schell, Ann Shanahan, Sam Sloan, Marian Stanley, Jim Symonds, Molly Theriault, Deb Thomas, Chris Turner, Virginia Vernon, Gaynelle Weiss, and Carol Williford all made a huge difference in how this work came together.

To my agent, Susan Lee Cohen of Riverside Literary Agency, herself a courageous free agent, I say thank you for your support and your patience with my roller-coaster process. The brilliant Carole DeSanti, editor extraordinaire at Penguin Putnam and inspired mentor, is also a dear friend and a major life blessing.

The good-humored support of the home team—Emerson and Thoreau, the comforting old tiger cats, and merry English springer spaniels Nell and Molly (who was birthed by Nell just after this book was conceived) and my partner, Sandy Lovejoy—has enabled me to laugh and feel well loved, the two most important things, throughout the writing process. As with my first book, Sandy has been there every step of the way, from considering the idea and editing again and again, to coaxing miracles out of the weary computer at the very last. Her belief in me and her willingness to do whatever it takes to make things happen is one of the essential ingredients of my own free agency.

CONTENTS

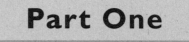

Part One

THE TIME IS NOW

> "The future is disorder. A door like this has cracked open five or six times since we got up on hind legs. It is the best possible time to be alive, when almost everything you knew is wrong."
>
> —Tom Stoppard

INTRODUCTION

--➤

Free to Succeed

"Don't compromise yourself. You're all you've got."

—Janis Joplin

People are tired of not being in charge of their own work lives—tired of wondering when the next merger might send them packing, tired of being forced to choose between their families and their careers, tired of being discriminated against because of their age, and tired of wanting desperately to use skills and interests that don't fit into their current jobs. Clearly, people are eager to *own their own lives,* but they're often not sure if that's really possible for them.

How happy are you really, *really,* to go to work each day, and how much control do you feel over your own life? If you're working the right number of hours and making enough money to meet your real needs; if you're feeling satisfied with the balance of your life; if your health and relationships are in good shape; if you have a plan in place for a reasonable retirement; and if you're pretty sure your employer will not be undergoing any major changes that will cost you your job or some benefits in the next several years, then this book is not for you. *You're also part of a very small minority of working adults.*

Or do any of the following statements have a jarring familiarity?

- "I finally know what I'd like to be doing, but nobody will pay me to do it."
- "I really want to carve out time for doing my own thing, but I also want to stay with my current employer. I feel crazy wanting to do both."
- "The field I'm in isn't anything like it was when I started, and I don't like what I see. If only I could do the things I want to do and still make a living."
- "I've never really found a job that fits me."
- "I was laid off six months ago and can't find anything in my field. Maybe nobody wants me because I'm over 50."
- "I just want more time for myself."
- "I'd love to go back to school, but I can't do that and pay the bills at the same time."
- "I started a business they said was hot several years ago and I'm not any happier than I was as an employee; what's wrong with me?"
- "My boss is on my case all the time, telling me I have to work longer hours and do more work. I really have to get out of here, but where could I go?"
- "The pension I was expecting to retire on has just been cut in half, and there's not a thing I can do about it."

All of these people are seriously compromising themselves because they haven't figured out how to design their own lives.

But more than 40 million Americans, over one-third of the workforce, already belong to a cohort of freedom-loving individuals known as "free agents." Futurists vary in their estimates of how fast free agency will grow (or even what scenarios are included in it), but most expect that within the decade somewhere between half and three-quarters of us, either *by default* (because other options have been closed off) or *by design* (because we decided to take control of our own careers) could be free agents in one way or another.

I hear many stories in coaching or counseling sessions from people who are experiencing their jobs as *enslaving,* with few options about controlling their own work lives. *Free agency is for workers of all kinds who'd like to take charge of their own careers.* To some analysts, free agency is limited to independent contractors and other entrepreneurs. My definition is much broader than that, and includes all of the following:

- Being self-employed on either a full-time or part-time basis, in a business or professional practice
- Supplementing your primary employment with partial self-employment (I call that a "sidecar")
- Making art of one kind or another, on a full- or part-time basis
- Working part-time or seasonally rather than in a "regular" full-time routine
- Flexing your employment contract to fit with your obligations or preferred rhythms, through telecommuting, variable schedules, home work, sabbaticals, and other special arrangements with your employer
- Working as an "intrapreneur" on your own special projects inside other people's organizations, with creative autonomy and the challenge of being responsible for what comes of your efforts
- Going to school or pursuing other interests in addition to your "regular" part-time or full-time work

More and more of us are determined to be free, if only for part of the work week. *It's time that we legitimized this need,* inside and outside of organizations.

The new free agency movement balances delicately on the following three legs:

1. The impact of technology and cyber-economics on how businesses and organizations run; the democratization of "possibilities" accomplished by internet access

2. The pressing need for work to be done in fluid motion, organized by tasks and projects rather than by clearly delineated and limiting job titles
3. People's desire to find meaning and self-expression in their lives, particularly in their mid-thirties and beyond

Some people have already discovered the thrill of the new "possibilities" which are abundant in e-commerce. They are fast-moving multitaskers, eager to trade off security for challenge and opportunity, even if that might mean failing once or twice along the way.

But many others lament the passing of the time when companies had a stable of workers slotted into discrete jobs—that they dared not leave, of course, because of the golden handcuffs or health insurance and pensions. Eighty-five percent of the millions of jobs lost to downsizing, reorganizing, and outsourcing in the past decade will never be resurrected. For some, that spells betrayal and fear. *But it doesn't need to be that way.*

I know because I've counseled and coached thousands of people to being more in control of their lives, in my role as director of career and executive development at Smith College and with my private clients. You see, I'm an incurable sidecar driver myself, having spent twenty-plus years developing a variety of auxiliary ventures, including counseling and coaching; consulting to corporations, small businesses, and nonprofits; working as the Career Coach on Monster.com; radio; and, of course, writing books and giving speeches. I know firsthand the thrill you get from figuring out how to put your own label on your work. I also know how terribly wrong and toxic it feels *not* to be making room in your life for the things that really matter to you. *My primary reason for writing this book, in fact, is to help those of you who might not think that the new free agent economy holds any special promise for you to see that it really does.* You can test-drive the idea here. Let me share with you what I and millions of workers have found to be true about the promise of free agency, in one form or another.

MAKING THE BAD NEWS GOOD

Free agency is as much a psychological as an economic phenomenon. "Free" is the key word here. It's about facing down your fears, being willing to take responsibility for yourself, in order to feel more in control of your own destiny. In many workplaces, employees are angry and depressed, mostly because they feel a lack of control over how they do their work. Free agency can *give you back the feeling of control you need to stay emotionally and physically healthy*.

Unfortunately, seeing the inevitability and the advantages of working freely is not the same as developing the strategies, skills, and attitudes to make it work for you. Psychologists who use the Myers-Briggs Type Indicator (MBTI) say, in fact, that nearly three-fourths of workers are temperamentally "wired" to eschew risk and ambiguity. Their fear of the unknown often keeps them stuck in stressful situations while their more nimble-minded colleagues dance away to new challenges and rewards.

The difference between staying on in a job that's making you miserable and taking yourself to free agency is *the ability to imagine alternatives*. But that's hard for many people. As Andrew Kimball observed in *The Utne Reader,* "We've worked so long at jobs we 'have to' that we often haven't considered the work we want and need to do." Perhaps you're among the many adults feeling bereft of ideas or more than a little anxious without some guarantees about their future.

Few of us were raised in families that prepared us for the "publicness" and self-determination of free agency. Mostly in our families and schools, we were primed for invisibility, for fitting in and not making waves. But the new free agent economy demands the opposite of us. The twenty-first century is asking us to dream more, risk a little more, and make our work fit into the rest of our lives, rather than vice versa.

Many who wondered at first whether they could survive (financially and emotionally) without the predictable ease of regular employment with one organization have discovered that the variety and stimulation of full or partial self-employment far outweigh the risks and problems. Even when they take a tumble, entrepreneurs, in fact, usually get back up on the horse and try again. Studies of workplace satisfaction show consistently that people who feel in charge of their own destiny are most likely to enjoy their work and do it well. That can happen for free agents who are on their own entirely. It also happens for those who have sidecar enterprises and for those who have found ways to work independently as employees within organizations. That's clearly what my clients are saying to me as well.

The new free agent economy also provides you with opportunities to fold more of your emotional and spiritual self into how you're spending your hours each week. When you "spend" your time doing the things that really matter to you, the "payoff" is tremendous. Some of you will figure out how to have all of your work closely aligned with what's most important to you. Others will work out a compromise plan, carving out time from your usual schedule to do additional work that expresses you in some important way. And, it's important to remember, work that's primarily unpaid at the beginning can *eventually* account for a much larger part (or even all) of your livelihood. No matter what your situation, navigating the changed work world of the twenty-first century, in ways that are both true to your internal compass and compatible with keeping a roof over your head, will be a challenge. But it's definitely possible.

Free to Succeed is meant to be read, put down, and then picked up again when you hit a rough spot. Like a wise friend, it can help you to discover *what you know, but don't know you know*—about yourself and about flourishing amid the twists and turns of the new free agent economy. Taking control of your own work life can lift you beyond your own uncertainty, as you feel yourself flying in unexpected but exciting directions. As the poet Mary Oliver observed, "When the thumb of fear lifts, we are so alive." You can get to where you really want to go, even if you don't yet know what that is.

CHAPTER ONE

New Economy Rules

"Forget jobs; look for the work that needs doing."
—William Bridges

"It's just not fair!" How many times have I heard that from people struggling to hold on to what's familiar in today's turbulent economy. In my office, on the phone, or via the internet, it comes to me on a daily basis, as millions of people fight back against the inevitability of the fact that the things they believed about the world of work may no longer be true for them. Harvard Business School professor Louis "By" Barnes once predicted, "Eventually, the organization will betray you." To displaced and unhappy workers, as they see contracts that were built on loyalty, reliability, and appreciation shattering all around them, this pronouncement seems on target. But not all experts believe that these changes are necessarily a problem. Canadian economist Nuala Beck asserts that "there's more than enough room in the New Economy to accommodate everyone. But first they need a proper road map to find their way." To draw that new map, let's look at what's really happening.

THE NEW CONTRACT

There's very little doubt about it—downsizing is here to stay. Despite the fact that downsizing has been likened to anorexia nervosa and has brought long-term increases in productivity and profitability for less than 25 percent of the organizations who have implemented it, in this economy of mergers and acquisitions, companies will very likely continue to overuse it. A major goal of many entrepreneurs is to grow and then sell their companies—which ensures that "redundancies" will keep on occurring. It's not even so unusual anymore for companies to lay off 10 to 40 percent of a unit's workforce in one fell swoop to respond to restructuring or market forces.

Similarly, the push for nonprofits and government entities to slim down and save money is having a domino effect. A study of the Michigan health care system, for instance, showed that a loss of 10,000 hospital jobs led to the disappearance of 7,000 jobs in other industries, which together cost $717 billion in lost salaries and wages and $1.1 billion in lost sales of goods and services.

Since 1979, millions of jobs have been jettisoned, and the trend is not expected to have run its course any time soon. One of the most difficult outcomes of this phenomenon is that fewer than one-third of men in their fifties and older who are downsized are likely to find similar jobs—the remaining two-thirds are the ones who send me plaintive on-line messages asking what has happened to make this perceived betrayal possible. Almost 60 percent of the *Fortune 500* have restructured in the past three years. More than one in three *Fortune 500* companies disappear every seven years. What's more, futurists like Tom Peters are predicting that within ten years, more than 90 percent of today's white collar "jobs" will have been eliminated or charred beyond recognition. Even now, there are many more qualified managers and executives than there are permanent positions available. The erosion of retirement and health insurance contracts has also taken many Americans by surprise. Employer willingness to carve away benefits that many workers thought were their due, combined with the bottom line–oriented value system of managed care, has left many people feeling adrift and vulnerable. Clearly, it's not a good time to be expecting your employer to take care of you.

It's easy to see why depression and rage are so much a part of American culture today. That is, of course, a catch-22. Longtime employees abandoned by their employers, only to find themselves unable to find similar work, do have a right to be angry. But they pay a huge price. Anger and resentment almost always get in the way of their thinking clearly enough to make good plans about their "next steps." These emotions usually undercut their desirability as candidates for employment as well. Interviewers can detect a chip on somebody's shoulder from across a room, and will almost always reject that person as "too negative, a potential troublemaker," even though the individual has just been ditched by an employer who once seemed to have promised a lifetime contract. The value of free agency in this situation is that *it offers a way to use your anger as a catalyst to create something new for yourself*—jet fuel for the trip rather than a can of lighter fluid for reigniting the fires of resentment every day. Moving from angry to energized is not as hard as it might seem!

Who's working?

The demographics of the workforce have shifted in important ways as well. As writer Tom Stewart pointed out in *Fortune* magazine, "The organization man did not die, he morphed . . . and he underwent a sex change too." In 1956, 85 percent of men worked, and 35 percent of women worked outside the home. Forty years later, 75 percent of men and 62 percent of women are working. Rosie the Riveter is back in spades, but this time she won't be sent home when the war is over! Here's the good news about gender. The prevalence of females in the workforce has caused many changes, some welcomed by men, some not. But new family-friendly norms in "coed" workplaces are indeed making it easier for both genders to get the flexibility they need to be free agents, on either a full-time or part-time basis.

Two other factors are also at work here. First, there are one million new widows each year. Many of those women will need to work and have not adequately prepared for becoming a solo wage earner. Where will they go? How will they be absorbed into a knowledge-based, youth-oriented work culture? What special skills and aptitudes might they be able to contribute? Secondly, 76 million of us are nearing what has traditionally been regarded as retirement age. But fewer than 3 percent of Americans have $50,000 put away for retirement. How will they live? Will they continue to work well into their seventies, as futurist Charles Handy predicts— Handy claims that we are well on our way to an average retirement age of 72. The answer to this spate of questions is, of course, that most of them will need to find ways to create their own work opportunities.

Where are people working?

That has changed too, as you probably know. In 1965, 20 percent of American workers were employed by *Fortune 500* companies. Now only 10 percent work in the *Fortune 500*. In the U.S., we now make more computers than cars, and the travel services business is larger than petroleum and steel combined. At the same time, there are four times as many workers involved in producing surgical and medical instruments as in all plumbing and heating products combined. We have become a nation of knowledge workers, with almost half of us working directly in knowledge-oriented industries, and the rest of us impacted by them in one way or another. As Tom Stewart observed, "The capital value of knowledge now exceeds the capital value of fixed assets in many corporations. . . . The worker is worth more than his tools."

Increasingly, business is also newer and smaller. More than one-third of American households have at least one person working out of a home office. A new business is born every eight seconds. Nearly half of American employers have fewer than 50 employees, and there are 41 million small enterprises in the United States with 51 million expected by 2002. Service-producing industries will account for nearly *all new job growth* in the next decade, and for the foreseeable future. Women-owned small businesses are the fastest-growing segment of the U.S. economy. Professional specialists plus service workers are expected to account for nearly half of employment opportunities in the next several years. This, of course, neatly sets the scene for the emergence of more and more free agents—the people whose temperament, skills, and aptitudes have positioned them perfectly to take advantage of this moment in our economic history. As economist Milton Friedman observed, "It is possible today to a greater extent than at any time in the world's history, for a company to locate anywhere, to use resources from anywhere, to produce a product that can be sold anywhere." But most of you will need some help in figuring out how to ride this wave successfully, to achieve the autonomy you want.

What are people hoping for?

In human affairs, it's always hard to sort out cause and effect. Chaos theorists, in fact, tell us that effects inevitably become causes. But, for whatever reason, American dreams seem to be shifting. Twenty years ago only a handful of MBA students wanted to become consultants; now consulting firms take away more than half the graduates of top business programs every spring. Among recent college graduates, 72 percent are telling pollsters that they want to own their own businesses someday. More than three-fourths of both men and women say they'd gladly trade money for time to be with their families and have a personal life. Articles about "the talent war" abound in business and mass market publications, with more and more companies being forced to allow for flexibility, telecommuting, part-time work, or seasonal assignments to attract and keep good people.

For many people, that's really good news. Much of my practice of counseling and performance coaching is now comprised of helping workers negotiate with their current employers to get more freedom for themselves. More than 98 percent of telecommuters, for instance, reported in a Wirthlin Worldwide poll that not only were they happier telecommuting, but they had seen general increases in worker morale because of it. The time has never been better for you to figure out what you need and ask for it. *The folks who are in trouble in the free agent economy are the ones too timid to imagine what more freedom might look like; too disorganized or uninformed to go after it in a strategic way; or not yet skilled enough to function effectively in technology-based environments.* Fortunately, all of those problems can be fixed.

STILL CHANGING—BUT TO WHAT?

For two decades my office has been filled with doctors, lawyers, judges, professors, senior executives, and college administrators, all confessing that they really don't like doing what they're good at anymore. That's hardly news. But what is different now is *the rate at which they're appearing*: That has escalated tremendously in the past five years. They are also less likely to be thinking of *just switching jobs or fields;* they are now much more likely to be considering a *major overhaul of how they're living their lives.* They're asking hard questions about meaning, quality of life, and autonomy. Not such a coincidence: Workplace America needs more highly skilled, nimble contingency workers, just at the same time that increasing numbers of people have begun to yearn to be more in charge of their own lives. If *adaptability-hungry employers* can figure out how to collaborate with *freedom-loving individuals,* the road to success may not be as elusive as it seems.

If you're willing to let go of the predictability of one regular full-time paycheck, the possibilities for earning your living by doing the work you love have never been greater. When you stop thinking "one employer and one job" and start thinking "work I can do for any number of organizations or individuals," either entirely on my own or as a sidecar, there is suddenly much more room to maneuver—you increase your *degrees of freedom* exponentially.

Consultant and author William Bridges suggests that we all should think of ourselves as a compendium of "microbusinesses," i.e., as multiple services we could deliver to a wide range of people. Match a skill or a quality of yours to a problem somebody (either an organization or an individual) needs to have solved, and with planning and forethought, you're in business!

WHO WILL MAKE IT AND WHO WON'T?

Chapters three and four consider both the "temperament" aspects of working on your own and the seven necessary steps to succeeding at free agency. First, let's look at *ten essential strategies for the new free agency economy:*

1. *Learn to tolerate ambiguity.* People who keep on needing to know what's going to happen before they're able to make a move will be left standing on the dock as the boat to the new economy pulls out. Coaching, counseling, reading, talking to people who are surviving without formal structures can all offer reassurance and help people develop this important attitude.

2. *Forget the old identity*. The U.S. is one of the few places where we assume that "we are what we do." Thus, Americans stay stuck in what they've been doing because to leave it would call into question their social and personal identities. The *tabula* must be *rasa* here, to open the door to new ways of doing things.

3. *Forget job descriptions and bosses*. The key to new economy success is imagining oneself as an independent purveyor of skills and services, eager to sell to the people who need or want them, even if only for part of the work week.

4. *Button the wallet and stash the credit cards*. Free agency requires a cautious relationship to money, at least at the beginning. Whatever doesn't get spent on "anesthetics" will provide many more degrees of freedom for designing a working life that doesn't require blocking out the pain of toxic work.

5. *Take back time*. Almost every schedule contains time that's currently being given away, with no real personal or professional return. Successful free agents assume that every expenditure of time is up for reevaluation as they prepare to launch.

6. *Save time for relationships*. The natural pull will be toward busy-ness and focusing on the tasks at hand. But research says very clearly that the best way to build resilience is to keep one's non-work relationships in tip-top condition.

7. *Develop skills or find help*. Computer skills, internet dexterity, foreign languages, quantitative skills, the ability to make cold calls or to market oneself shamelessly, tolerance for new and different kinds of people, bookkeeping and organizational skills—the list is seemingly endless. But you have three choices here: (1) do these things yourself, (2) partner with someone

who has complementary skills, or (3) hire someone to do them. They just can't be ignored. The trick is to put one's own energies where they're needed most. As business professor Deborah Burke observed, "Doing the wrong low-value tasks can kill a free agent."

8. *Remember the bigger picture.* Free agents don't have the luxury of not knowing what's happening in domestic and international markets or of not knowing about trends in their own and related fields. Thankfully, the internet makes it easier than it was even several years ago to stay on top of things, and hence make the right anticipatory moves.

9. *Get a gang.* Whether it's a writers' group, some like-minded folks at your local chamber of commerce, a free agent networking group on the web, a purchasing collaborative, a professional or supervision group, or any other kind of formal or informal association, the support of others is essential. One of the most compelling examples of an effective "gang" is the Renaissance Entrepreneurship Center in San Francisco. In the ten years that this organization has been helping to launch new ventures, more than 87 percent of the businesses started there are still in operation, quadruple the national average for new business success. What's more, 60 percent of their businesses do business with each other. It's a "sticking together" model that really seems to work.

10. *Find a coach.* Without a boss to provide marching orders, free agents need someone to lean on as they navigate through choppy waters. Times of transition usually bring to the surface every other crisis, uncertainty, or change you've ever endured. A coach can help figure it all out, with insights about what's current and what's old news that should be put to rest. The coach should be someone who understands free

agency, is informed about your field, and builds your confidence. The last thing any free agent needs is yet another disapproving authority figure.

The people who will have trouble in the new economy, and who will then cry "foul" the loudest, are the ones who choose not to take steps to turn these changes into opportunities for themselves. *But the blame will be theirs*. Admittedly, today's economy fits more easily with some personalities and temperaments than with others. But "free agent thinking" is an attitude everyone can learn.

There will indeed still be some "old century" work around in the new millennium, and so people trying to "hold on for a while" will be able to dig up evidence that there's no need to be thinking about change. But the only way to feel secure (not *job security*, remember, but *personal security*), is to be ready to take care of yourself, no matter what might happen. There's really no place to hide. It took nearly 40 years for "blue collar robots" in factories and heavy-duty work sites to accomplish the unraveling of assumptions about how physical work gets done. The "white collar robots" in offices are expected to make "middle people" and paper pushers mostly obsolete in less than ten. A decade ago, the practice of planning ahead for your own future, rather than relying on your employer to push you up the ladder toward success, was called "employability" by management gurus and human resources specialists. Now it's just called common sense.

FREE AGENTS WITHIN ORGANIZATIONS

"Free agent" encompasses not just entrepreneurs, but all workers—including those inside organizations—*who are choosing to exert more control over how their work gets done*. Telecommuters (almost 20 million of them), flex-timers, moonlighters, part-time students, for instance, are all *taking liberties* with that "gray flannel suit" nine-to-five (or nine-to-nine) contract. They're daring to say "This is what would work better for me, and so I know *it* would benefit the organization too." And you know what? *It will be better for the organization!*

Research shows clearly that workers who are given control over how they do their work not only stay healthier, but are more productive and effective as well. A *Harvard Business Review* article discussed employees' "deeply imbedded life interests." The authors argued that it's essential for managers to know what motivates their workers, so they can help them manifest these drives (such as communicating, deal-making, technology, theory development, creativity, or coaching others) in their work, one way or the other. Authors Butler and Waldroop, as well as many other experts, are saying clearly to organizations: *Find out what matters to your people, and make a way for them to have it.* Is this because corporate America has had an attack of altruism? No. It's because one of the biggest problems facing American business is the talent shortage, the inability to find and keep people with the attitudes, skills, knowledge, and commitment to work effectively in the new economy. And it has become clear that catering to employee motivations and needs is one of the best ways to keep the people employers need most. If you're someone who'd like to combine the stability of those payroll checks with a little more autonomy and self-directedness, now is just the right time for you to ask about it.

SEIZE THE MOMENT

Free agents within organizations, take note: Ask for what you need. Here are some of the arrangements my clients and colleagues have negotiated in the past several years. Some have to do with managing your schedule more to your own liking, while others are about adding new dimensions to your work.

- Flex time: four-day weeks, staggered work times, coming late or leaving early as necessary
- Reduced schedules: working less than full-time at the job, usually saving the employer money in the process, because auxiliary help can be brought in at a cheaper rate
- Overlapping projects: permission to work on projects that benefit both you and the organization because of some overlap in mission
- Job sharing
- Time and tuition benefits to get trained in a new functional area
- Assignments in different work units to get a broader perspective on a field or industry
- Freedom to work out of the office on projects that require special concentration
- Intrapreneuring: creating a start-up venture as an employee of the company and then eventually taking it out on your own
- Working in two positions at once: blending an old job with a new one
- Doing multiple jobs simultaneously or in sequence
- Taking on projects or responsibilities that are new for the organization, so you learn new skills or product knowledge, and "practice launch" ventures without risking your own resources
- Working on task forces or ad hoc teams, in addition to your regular job

Now, your boss is never going to waltz up and offer you these freedoms, you know. But if any of them sound right to you, read on—and learn how to position yourself to go and ask for what you need. Here's one thing to remember about asking, however: *Any idea you present must be couched in terms of "why this is good for the organization" rather than just a need of yours.* Usually, that's pretty easy to do. What could possibly be "in it" for your employer to give you the flexibility you want right now? Here are just a few things, some of which might well fit your situation:

- Increased productivity due to decreased distractions
- Lower costs for space or equipment
- Reduced absenteeism or turnover
- Improved worker morale and health
- Reduced travel costs/time
- Increased responsiveness to queries from different time zones, outside of a rigid nine-to-five framework
- Access to part-time or retired workers to round out the labor pool
- Ability to vary work hours in response to pressing deadlines or unexpected crises
- Most important, keeping you on board instead of losing you or your enthusiasm

By asking for what will work for you, in terms that emphasize the benefit to your employer, you can make your own deeply imbedded life interests a major part of your work. To help you out, you might want to copy this section and place it on the boss's desk, or suggest that this chapter in the book be discussed at a unit meeting.

Bosses in organizations, listen up: Don't make it hard for the folks who come to you asking for some of these "freedoms." Here's the main reason why—*the people who yearn for some elbow room in their lives are probably the ones you need the most.* They are the ones who can imagine different lives for themselves and, therefore, see different possibilities for your product line or organization. They are the innovators and risk-takers you need in order to survive and thrive. If you cut them off at the knees when they gather up the courage to ask for what they need, you're going to lose them anyway— if not physically, then in spirit for sure. More than 80 percent of successful entrepreneurs, for instance, reported in one study that they had first offered their innovative idea to their bosses, but were turned away. With luck and some careful listening on your part, you might be able to offer them enough flexibility and freedom for them to stay with you and do the other things that matter to them on the side. Do yourselves a big favor, and don't chase away your best hope to succeed in the new free agent economy.

Dee Hock, founder of one of the first successful "free floating" corporations, Visa International, had some important advice for workers and employers alike: ". . . the Buddhists got it half right with their doctrine of reincarnation. Reincarnation exists. What they got wrong is the belief you have to die first. You can be reborn in your lifetime."

CHAPTER TWO

------------------------------ →

It's Good for Me—Is It Good for You?

"I'm completely fed up with Dilbert. He's funny. He's unerringly on the money. But he's a hapless victim. Damned if I'm going to be."

—Tom Peters

Sports idol Wayne Gretzky was once asked, "What makes you a great hockey player?" He responded, "I go where the puck is going to be, not where it is." Anticipating where the new economy puck will end up has become the responsibility of all of us—at least all of us who would like to be earning a living for the foreseeable future.

For most of us, the "puck" is not going to be in the land of paternalistic (or maternalistic) companies who will reward their long-term, ever-loyal employees with lavish perks and unassailable job security. There will be lavish corporate perks for some, but by no means for the majority of workers. And the folks getting those perks will not have any guarantee that they'll be where the puck is either in a month or a year. In fact, says Canadian economist Nuala Beck, "If you're employed in the old economy, you have a better than 50 percent chance of losing your job."

For most of us, the "puck" is pretty much guaranteed to be in the land of free agency, that sometimes hard-to-imagine place where people expect to take care of themselves, in one way or another, in return for having control over how things get done. For some of you, the ones with credentials and confidence and technical skills that put you on the "right side" of the digital divide, taking care of yourselves shouldn't be that hard. For others it will be harder—not impossible, but just a little tougher.

Free agency, of course, comes in varying styles. Some entrepreneurs are in it to "go for broke." These people with "high-growth" intentions make the rounds of venture capitalists looking for angel investors. They remortgage their houses and borrow from friends and relatives to get the capital they need to make a splash with their new venture. Their goal is to make it big. Perhaps that's you—or somebody you care about—even though one study showed that only 3 percent of new entrepreneurs planned to take their companies public eventually.

Others start small with the intention of staying small and manageable. Enterprises like these have been called "lifestyle" ventures, because they're intended to create a reasonable living for the individual and perhaps a few family members or close associates. But it's not the owner's intention to explode onto the economic scene and risk everything. Unfortunately, *many people seem wary of free agency because they picture it only as the first form—a big deal, high-risk adventure.* There is tremendous variety in the way free agents approach their ventures. The average venture capital funding for a new business is $200,000. Those who get a good start with a new business, particularly a technical one, will then go back for millions more. But the majority of the new businesses or practices launched each year are much more modest in scope. You could, for instance, start a cleaning service or pet care business with less than $1,000 and be making enough to pay your bills in six months to a year. If you wanted to start a consulting or accounting practice requiring communication equipment and advertising, it would probably take $10,000 if you could work out of your own home. In all these "lifestyle" cases, the ideal way to start might be to begin slowly with a sidecar venture. That's very different from what you'd need to do in a high-growth situation, where getting a fast, well-resourced start often makes the difference between succeeding and failing. Free agency ventures are just like the people who start them—infinitely varied. One size strategy will definitely not fit all. The trick is to choose the style that works for you in terms of time, resources, visibility, debt load, risk, and potential. The "Risk Continuum" exercise in Part Three can help you see a little more clearly where you might fit.

WHAT'S IN IT FOR EMPLOYERS?

Well, that's a no-brainer, you're probably saying. Organizations get permission to use people up, avoid expensive benefits, and then let workers go at the drop of a hat. Why shouldn't they want lots of us hanging around waiting to be called to work? Watch out—*that's a victim mentality speaking,* and *it's not going to help you.* This is not about robbing you of what's owed you, but rather about your changing how you understand the employer-employee contract in the context of today's faster-moving, highly technical, global marketplace.

Obviously, it's advantageous for companies to be able to exercise flexibility and be responsive to market shifts—to be able to deploy forces in areas where they're needed rather than keep people where they're under-utilized. AT&T, for instance, saved nearly $500 million through "alternative officing" away from company sites, while at Nortel the shift to having 4,000 workers telecommute increased productivity by 24 percent in one year. Unfortunately, shifting gears in an organization, asking people to retrain to be able to do tomorrow's tasks or to work differently, is all too often regarded by workers as another burden imposed from on high—rather than as an opportunity to stay challenged and vital. But with a variety of differently skilled workers (i.e., independent ven-

dors of talent, skills, and knowledge) to choose from, much
time, money, and angst can be saved.

Organizations would definitely benefit from the improve-
ments in worker morale and productivity that often come
with flexibility for workers. Ninety percent of organizations
that offer flex-time, for instance, reported that worker attitudes changed for the better, even among those workers not
electing to use it. Studies also show conclusively that people
who are learning more stay healthier, happier, and more effective than those who have settled into a routine of "how we
do it here." This has long-term impact on the bottom line. It's
estimated, in fact, that the stress of having employees doing
work they don't like in ways they don't want to do it is currently costing employers up to $750 per worker each year.

There are also proven financial advantages to having virtual rather than on-site workers. In one analysis of the costs
of processing *one insurance application,* for instance, these
were the startling results:

- Cost of processing a policy with traditional sequential,
  on-site individual workers, moving papers from desk to
  desk: 2 weeks time/$1,000
- Cost of processing with high-performing, coordinated
  team effort: 1 week/$900
- Cost of processing online by a virtual team of contract
  workers/experts: 30 minutes/$100

Is there any doubt, then, that employers will be wanting
workers to increase their technical skills to be able to par-
ticipate in this revolution? By making ongoing learning the
province of the *employee* as well as the *employer,* employers
are ensured a much more vital and engaged pool of workers.
And workers themselves are much less likely to experience
emotional and physical ailments that cost them and their employers in the long run.

At the same time, having the freedom to choose from among

a variety of workers makes it much more likely that employers can find the talent they need to stay competitive and deliver on what they've promised to their customers. This is not necessarily bad news for workers either—since they are then free to negotiate as vendors for the compensation, flexibility, and working conditions they want.

WHAT'S IN IT FOR WORKERS?

The news is good for employers, but it's even better for those workers who do what's necessary to keep themselves marketable. Wouldn't you like to have the following seven benefits of free agency in your life now?

1. *Greater sense of control over your work life.* People who contract with organizations and individuals to deliver services or products have the same bargaining power as other vendors. There's more risk, but there's also more control.

2. *Greater work satisfaction.* Even though self-employed people frequently work more hours than employees, they report greatly enhanced levels of pleasure in their work. In a study of engineers, the self-employed almost always felt that what they were accomplishing was worthwhile, while "company-owned" engineers felt that way only about half the time. Company engineers also felt tired and overworked much more frequently than self-employed ones, even though they were working fewer hours than free agents.

3. *Better mental and physical health.* When you feel you're in control of things (and hence less stressed), every system in your body is happier. Your immune system deploys more NK and T-cell troops to combat infections. Your cardiovascular system is less likely to pump little globules of fat into your bloodstream. You are less

likely to have damaging stress hormones like cortisol racing through your body. Your endocrine system finds it easier to keep your emotions in balance. And your musculoskeletal system is able to work more effectively, without painful tension or spasms in your muscles. Ask any chiropractor about the relationship between work-induced stress and lower back pain.

4. *Burnout prevention.* There actually are several varieties of burnout being passed around in the workplace these days. One kind comes from feeling that you have too much to do in too little time—either because your manager is an ogre (and did you know that one-third of us work for people we regard as impossible?) or because your own boundaries are too loose. It's shocking, in fact, how many of us contribute to our own state of overwhelm by making poor decisions about how to use our time.

    The other variety of burnout happens when the juice has gone out of your work for you, and everything seems like a burden because it just doesn't interest you. And then an enduring fatigue sets in. Free agency, whether it's something you do full-time or part-time, can keep you out of the burnout ward.

5. *Potential for a more balanced life.* What if you were the only one telling you that you had to work late tonight? To be sure, entrepreneurs, freelancers, and other free agents often work intensely to get a big project done or meet a deadline. But then when it's done, if they've planned well enough and kept their boundaries well protected, they have the freedom to take the recuperative time they need, without asking anybody's permission. It's hard to put a price tag on that kind of flexibility—in fact, more than three-quarters of both men and women workers say they'd trade almost anything to get more of it.

6. *Protection against age discrimination.* You're 67 and you feel terrific—but nobody will hire you! I can't tell you how often I run into that scenario on my online message board and in counseling sessions. Age discrimination is the most wasteful by-product of our youth-culture economy. I'm convinced, however, that for people with skills and ideas to sell to meet other people's needs, this can truly be "an opportunity brilliantly disguised as a problem." If you're a free agent marketing a product or service that you enjoy providing, no 20-something hiring manager can ever tell you that you're too old!

7. *Ability to set your own retirement agenda.* Some folks want to retire early. Others never want to retire. The majority of us will choose something in the middle, reducing our total working hours gradually over the course of twenty years or so. Many people start in their forties or fifties to build a sidecar venture that will gradually become their primary income generator. Many artists, writers, and musicians have started doing their own work in earnest just as they were approaching retirement age. Twenty percent of the current workforce will hit retirement age by 2010. According to Yankelovich Partners, a research firm that monitors social trends, more than half of baby boomers are interested in starting a new career when they "retire."

Some of those in a new career will be there because they want to stay active and try new things. Others either "forgot" to save or could never see their way beyond some combination of limited opportunity and financial fumbles to have a few bucks to put aside. Whatever the reason, there are lots of folks sixty and over for whom giving up work is just not on the agenda anytime soon.

But if you're approaching retirement age and feeling "used

up" rather than energized about new ideas, listen to this: A study of people ages 65 to 102 showed that more than half of the subjects had had their best, most productive years after age 50, and that a whopping one-third of them had their most creative and enjoyable work experiences after age 65. There's no reason why you couldn't arrange to be your own boss and have your best years after 65 too!

WHAT'S IN IT FOR SOCIETY?

Not just companies and individuals will benefit from making it easier for people to become free agents in one way or another. Society can win too. As a culture of interdependent citizens, we need to pay attention to what could bring the greatest good for more of us. All of the following five desirable outcomes are possible (and even likely) when people are really prepared to make the most of this new free agent economy:

1. *Greater employment equity.* It's a sad fact that many employees are still having trouble being rewarded fairly for their talents and effort because of biases about gender, race, religion, social class, or sexual orientation. But when you're the boss, if you're savvy, planful, and hardworking, chances are other people's prejudices won't affect your ability to succeed at whatever level you choose. For instance, the work that pioneer Joline Godfrey, author of *Our Wildest Dreams* and founder of An Income of Her Own, is doing, teaching adolescent girls entrepreneurial skills, will in the long run have a tremendous impact on their ability to be independent and self-supporting. They will be much less likely to be undercompensated for their work and/or undervalued in their personal lives. That can only be good for society.

2. *Fuller employment/reduced unemployment costs.* In the long run, nobody benefits from a world split into haves and have-nots. The costs, both financial and personal, of keeping the majority of us from being able to earn a real living are astronomical. The delicate economic balance between corporate profit and unemployment has never settled out in favor of the little guy, and it's doubtful that it ever will. Free agency offers a way to keep more people autonomous and earning in mobile, flexible, and more enjoyable ways.

3. *Less disruption of family life.* The cumulative effect of employers requiring their workers to value workplace obligations over family responsibilities is devastating to workers and their families. But when *you're your own employer,* in one way or another, you can set rules that manage to keep the ship afloat, yet honor your personal responsibilities and keep your family strong.

4. *Less hopelessness and the accompanying social costs.* So what happens to people who want to work but can't get a foot in the door anywhere? I talk to thousands of them via my online message board, counseling sessions, and workshops each year. I can tell you that their angst is costing us (as well as them) a tremendous amount in depression and anxiety, substance abuse, domestic violence, child abuse, juvenile poverty rates, and even homelessness. But when people are helped to develop their own ventures, large or small, it's like the sun bursting out on a drizzly, gloomy day! Three-quarters of U.S. businesses are sole proprietorships, and hence a model for people from all walks of life hoping to find work that feeds them and provides dignity. Millions of people are out there ready to work who, for one reason or another, are being snubbed by credentials-crazed and youth-obsessed corporations. There's no reason for us to let large corporations set a

tone that keeps so many willing workers feeling that there is no place for them.

5. *Lower health care costs.* Work-related stress is still the number one health problem for working adults. Illness costs employers in terms of absenteeism and lost productivity, as well as in increased services which they underwrite in one way or another. Self-employed people who have figured out how to manage the ambiguity and keep their ventures on track, in fact, are probably the healthiest folks among us. Given the involuntary intermingling of our fates through the managed care system, that saves everybody money.

THE SPECIAL ADVANTAGES OF DRIVING A SIDECAR

A sidecar is a service or venture you launch without, as they say, "giving up your day job." You find the time somehow—evenings, weekends, vacation days, or by taking some unpaid time. Clearly, it's good for both employees and employers to allow people the freedom they need to develop their ventures gradually, rather than forcing them to leap all at once without benefit of paycheck into a new identity. When employers' policies, such as rigid control over employees' activities, no flexibility about hours or contracts, and the like, make it impossible for their best workers to experiment with doing their own thing on the side, then everybody loses.

But when organizations are smart enough to encourage their people to incubate their own projects, then everybody wins. The gain for workers is easy: They can build their ideas slowly, allowing for their evolution and fine-tuning. They get to keep their jobs, either full-time or part-time (preferably the latter to give the venture a reasonable start). They also avoid the mental and physical discomforts that are the inevitable result of feeling imprisoned full-time in a job and not allowed to give birth to one's dreams. *More than 80 percent of new businesses, in fact, begin as somebody's second job.*

In counseling sessions, I usually ask people to imagine their work life as divided into four quadrants. "Imagine," I suggest, "that your current job took up only two of the four quadrant spaces in your work life; what could you imagine doing with the other two?" Seldom do I get blank stares. Most people are off and running with possibilities before I've finished writing the name of their current employer on two of the quadrants I've drawn out in front of them. But here's the thing—unless you give yourself permission to imagine that the job you currently have doesn't need to take up your entire work life, then it will never occur to you to move the parts around and see what might happen. Who knows, if you built your love of graphics design into a sidecar design service in one quadrant and your fascination with computers into learning new programming language in another, you might end up eventually combining the two into a web design and management business. Then you'd have a choice about leaving your current job altogether to do your own business full-time, or keeping it a sidecar and having the best of both worlds.

One way to look at sidecars is as a way to transition *gradually* to where you want to be next. The diagram on the next page describes Cindy's progression from a full-time corporate trainer to an external consultant. Over five years, she decreased her time in the HR unit of her corporation until, in her fourth year, she was specializing in one kind of training, selling her services two days a week to her former employer. From year five on, she did occasional trainings at the "home" company, but was able to find many of her independent jobs through long-term relationships with people she had initially met when she was a full-time corporate trainer.

Even though the sidecar notion is sometimes a hard sell for old-economy bosses, the best news is that organizations benefit spectacularly too. They get to keep their key people,

THE GRADUAL TRANSITION GRID

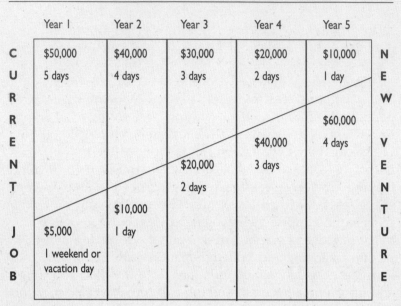

	Year 1	Year 2	Year 3	Year 4	Year 5	
C	$50,000	$40,000	$30,000	$20,000	$10,000	**N**
U	5 days	4 days	3 days	2 days	1 day	**E**
R						**W**
R					$60,000	
E				$40,000	4 days	**V**
N			$20,000	3 days		**E**
T			2 days			**N**
		$10,000				**T**
J	$5,000	1 day				**U**
O	1 weekend or					**R**
B	vacation day					**E**

the creative, energetic ones who think ahead and need challenges and change of pace. Frequently, they also get a bargain. One experienced craftsman named Dan, for instance, asked for a change to a three-day-per-week job with the up-scale renovation company where he worked, so that he could develop his own small antiques business on the side. At first his boss was worried that his mind would be on antiques rather than on the expert finishing work on which the company relied. But Dan was able to convince him that, with the savings the company would get from Dan's reduced rate of pay, they'd be able to hire an apprentice. Dan could then train his own eventual replacement and still allow the company to save money. "Besides," Dan pointed out, "would you rather have me for the three or so years it will take me to get this business up and running, or have me leave anytime now because my heart is at least partially someplace else?"

Of course, people with sidecar ventures don't always leave their primary employers. I have many clients and colleagues who've been doing things they really love on the side for years, because that enables them to stay contentedly in jobs where the bucks and the health insurance reside. By responding positively to requests like Dan's, employers can avoid the situation that shows up so often in my office— people who desperately want to start something on their own but yet, for one reason or another, can't afford to (or just don't wish to) cut loose from the mother ship. Many of them would be happy to continue on successfully with their jobs, so long as they had a little flexibility to explore their passions on the side. So they ask for flex-time or a reduced schedule and, when it's denied, just stay on, defeated, and pretty much retire on the job. As one senior female executive in the auto industry told me, "I know it works to give people permission to design their work lives to their own liking, but I can promise you that the boys at the top still don't get it."

That's too bad. What a different result could occur, for more people and for organizations, if their bosses had the presence of mind to allow them the flexibility they're seeking and in return get employees who are alive with the energy of learning and starting new things. If that were the case, we might not find in polls that 90 percent of workers would really rather be someplace else, if not in a new field, then at least in a different setting.

DIFFERENT STROKES FOR DIFFERENT FOLKS?

One of the most important outcomes of the new free agent economy can be loosening the stranglehold of traditional thinking that so often keeps people from making creative choices for themselves. We are meant to dream, to try new things, to revisit some of our adolescence at midlife, and to make courageous leaps into the unknown from time to time. As the late Charles Schulz observed, "Life is like a ten-speed bicycle. Most of us have gears we never use." The wonderful thing about these chaotic times is that the possibilities are there now, if we can once and for all acknowledge them and reject those scripts written for other players in other circumstances. Whether you'll ever want to be a free agent or not, the fact that you *could be if you chose to* is one of the most liberating things about being alive at the beginning of the twenty-first century.

CHAPTER THREE

-------------------------------- →

What Kind of Free Agent Would You Be?

"The world needs your creativity. Now is the time for you to make your unique contribution."

—Justine and Michael Toms

So what if you did decide that the freedom we've been discussing is something you'd like to have more of in your life? How could you tell in advance what this might be like for you? Let me tell you, free agents are definitely not all wired the same way. In the past several years, I've noticed six different types of would-be free agents. Some are interested in never again having to work for a boss. Some just want to be sure that they get to pursue their own creative ideas. Some want lots of time freedom and are willing to make less to march to their own drum. Still others are desperate for more money. Everybody has a particular style, or a combination of styles, and a unique story about where those preferences might lead them.

It's helpful to know in advance what kind of free agent you might be. This gives you affirmations about your *natural strengths* and a heads-up about some of the *obstacles you're likely to create for yourself*. The *Free Agency Motivator Inventory* that follows has helped many people figure out how free agency might work best for them, and how to manage the "weak links" in their chains. Try on the 42 statements that follow in the *FAMI,* and get a handle on what your free agency motivators might be.

FREE AGENT MOTIVATOR INVENTORY

Put a check in the column that describes you best. Then put the corresponding number in the final column, and add them up to get your score for that group.

Group One	(0) Not at all like me	(1) Somewhat like me	(2) Like me	(3) Very much like me	Number
I like to do things my way.					
Bosses are often bad news for me.					
I love to bend the rules when I can.					
I am my own person.					
Working for somebody else just doesn't do it for me.					
When people try to boss me around, I split or tune out.					
I pretty much say what's on my mind.					
Group One Total					

Group Two	(0) Not at all like me	(1) Somewhat like me	(2) Like me	(3) Very much like me	Number
People call me a daydreamer.					
I need variety and change of pace in my work.					
I often make decisions based on the mood I'm in.					
Flexibility is really important to me.					
I like for things to be spontaneous.					
I'm attracted to creative or artistic things.					
I'm more interested in making big plans than in the details.					
Group Two Total					

Group Three

	(0) Not at all like me	(1) Somewhat like me	(2) Like me	(3) Very much like me	Number
I have more creative ideas than I know what to do with sometimes.					
I can almost always think of new ways to do things.					
I see more connections between different things than other people seem to.					
I enjoy coming up with novel solutions to problems.					
Sometimes I have a hard time prioritizing my many ideas.					
I love learning about as many fields and ideas as I can.					
I like to have a lot of things going at once.					
Group Three Total					

Group Four	(0) Not at all like me	(1) Somewhat like me	(2) Like me	(3) Very much like me	Number
Taking chances excites me.					
I'd risk it all to make it big.					
I really want the money I make to reflect how hard I've worked; I'll do what it takes to make that happen.					
I'll make whatever sacrifices it takes to reach my goals.					
Money and/or fame are important to me.					
I don't like to be around overly cautious people.					
When I get an idea, I like to go with it, rather than spend a lot of time researching and planning.					
Group Four Total					

Group Five	(0) Not at all like me	(1) Somewhat like me	(2) Like me	(3) Very much like me	Number
I want my work to be manageable—to leave time and space for the other things that really matter to me.					
I'm not interested in money or achievements. Quality of life counts more for me.					
It's important to me to make time for more introspective, spiritual, or artistic activities.					
Taking care of my relationships is more important to me than financial success.					
Making time for community activities and personal commitments to others is as important to me as my paid work.					
I need a lot of quiet time to think and reflect.					
I couldn't do work that doesn't reflect my values.					
Group Five Total					

Group Six	(0) Not at all like me	(1) Somewhat like me	(2) Like me	(3) Very much like me	Number
I'm doing (or thinking about doing) my own thing, either full-time or on the side, because I need more money than I can make at my regular job.					
I don't have the credentials (either education or experience) to get hired full-time by someone else to do what I want to do— so I'm thinking about doing it (or am already doing it) on my own.					
I'm developing (or already have) a venture of my own, in order to be able to afford the things that matter to me.					
Financially, I'm in a "catch-up" mode.					
I want or need to work past regular retirement age.					
I'm working hard to pay off my debts.					
I'm doing (or thinking about doing) my own thing because there just don't seem to be any jobs that fit me now.					
Group Six Total					

What does your profile look like?   Using the scores for each group, color in each box up to the number of your score to indicate the relative strength of each group for you. (The chart will then look something like a bar graph.) Because some of you are "high estimators" while others are "low estimators," generally it's not the raw numbers that count, but rather their relationship to each other. Where are your highs and lows?

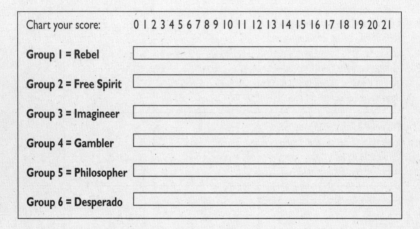

Chart your score:	0 1 2 3 4 5 6 7 8 9 10 11 12 13 14 15 16 17 18 19 20 21
Group 1 = Rebel	
Group 2 = Free Spirit	
Group 3 = Imagineer	
Group 4 = Gambler	
Group 5 = Philosopher	
Group 6 = Desperado	

What if you didn't score above 10 in any of the type groups?   It might mean that you're either not very motivated to be a free agent, or afraid of taking the risks and enduring the ambiguity involved. *But that doesn't mean you can't succeed if you decide you want to.* It just means you'd need to develop some of the qualities that seem to come more naturally to people who fall into one of those six groups. It could also be good news because you might not need to do as much "correcting" as some other people, should you decide to add some free agency to your life.

Correcting? You bet! *Your weaknesses are almost always the excesses of your strengths.* This means that, to be successful with your own brand(s) of free agency, you'll need to learn to capitalize on your strengths and rein in the excesses.

Perhaps you have two, three, or even four strong free agency motivators. That just means that you have more free agent aptitudes (and more potential hassles) to work with. Let's look at how all this plays out in practice.

GROUP #1: REBELS

So you're really interested in doing things your way. I bet you gave those elementary school teachers a run for their money. And if you went to Catholic school, you probably sent a few nuns off to their final reward a little early. Your lack of fear in most situations means that you'll probably be a good risk-taker. You're also probably a straight shooter, not hemmed in by fears of displeasing others. You'll make a great free agent. Free agency might seem to have been invented for you, in fact. But you can also run into difficulty if you don't curb some of your natural anti-authoritarian impulses.

GOOD NEWS FOR REBELS

- You have great energy—all that suppressed resistance to authority can be channeled into working hard for yourself or for what you believe in.
- You're a natural problem-solver, willing to break the rules to be successful. People will also probably feel that they know where they stand with you.
- You're likely to be very resourceful, and can usually think of side-door approaches when the front door is locked and you don't have a key.

POTENTIAL PROBLEMS AND ANTIDOTES FOR REBELS

- Your strong suit is probably not conflict resolution—so get some coaching or instruction there. Even when you're

the boss, you won't be able to avoid negotiating sticky
situations.

- Because you're used to doing things your way, it might
  be hard for you to listen to necessary feedback—
  and thus you can miss out on some essential course-
  correction information. Do whatever you can to learn to
  see feedback as your friend, intended to help you grow,
  rather than as an enemy.
- Your need to be right might cloud your judgment sometimes. Try to get your ego out of the way when important decisions need to be made. Trusted friends
  or a coach might be helpful in assessing tricky situations.

GROUP #2: FREE SPIRITS

As a budding free spirit, you must have chased a lot of
butterflies when you were a kid, and now you're still in-
tent on not getting hemmed in. Nine-to-five-times-five probably seems like an indeterminate prison sentence to you.
The volatile world of e-commerce and the unpredictability
of the current economy would probably suit you well—
you're definitely a grab-the-brass-ring type. Free agency is
a great match for free spirits like you, so long as you're careful to get some help building in the structure you'll need to
stay on track to be able to deliver on your contracts and
promises.

GOOD NEWS FOR FREE SPIRITS

- You have tons of new ideas for new ventures—somehow ideas seem to fly to you as you scan the horizon
  or tune in to what's happening around you. You'll also
  do well at integrating new discoveries and new ideas
  into your business, your practice, or your craft.

- You're really flexible, and able to shift as circumstances do, a necessary component of a market-sensitive concept like free agency.
- You're very likely to have a creative, artistic bent that you mustn't let slip away. It can serve you well, either directly or indirectly.

POTENTIAL PROBLEMS AND ANTIDOTES FOR FREE SPIRITS

- Watch out for overload—agreeing to do more than you can deliver on is probably a lifelong proclivity for you. It can really sink your ship when your success depends on customers or clients knowing that they can count on you to do what you say you will. A terrific assistant or advisor with a good "operations head" will probably be a necessity.
- Focusing on the task at hand might be hard for you, as it is for most multitasking individuals. Lack of structure and concentration almost always leads to scattered and disappointing results. Free spirits have a tendency to let their work spaces, their thoughts, and their lives get cluttered, which in turn costs them momentum. Ask that great assistant of yours to help here too.
- Talents that aren't developed begin to "itch" as you get older. If you have them, you'd better begin to find some outlets for them, or they'll make you frustrated and, eventually, depressed. Have you been putting off doing what you really want to do? If yes, find someone, perhaps a friend, family member, or counselor, to help you figure out a plan for making it happen.

GROUP #3: IMAGINEERS

If you're an imagineer, I bet you're fun to be around—because your brain seldom shuts down. You probably drove your teachers crazy asking questions that never occurred to anyone else, and I suspect your adolescence was no picnic for your parents. You love information and you love putting together all different kinds of facts and ideas—your mind is kaleidoscopic, in fact. But watch out what you do with all that creative thinking; taking it to market in a way that keeps you out of the land of disappointment can be harder than you think.

GOOD NEWS FOR IMAGINEERS

- You're a natural-born innovator, and so you'll often be able to figure out novel solutions to problems, for yourself or as a consultant or troubleshooter for others.
- You see the connections that others don't. Capitalize on that ability to identify patterns and relationships in what seems like a speeded-up, disjointed world to many.
- Your intellectual ebullience is attractive to people looking for help, or for a place to invest their money. You can be sure that, in the creative ideas department, "there's plenty more where this came from."

POTENTIAL PROBLEMS AND ANTIDOTES FOR IMAGINEERS

- Keep your feet on the ground at least a little bit while your head's in the clouds, or you'll never get those ideas launched. Get some help designing organizational and delivery systems that don't require you to be paying attention to them all the time.
- You must find a way to get the conservative and practical advice you need, to be able to sort out the wild ideas that can succeed from the ones that are bound to flop. Get yourself a residential pessimist to help you spot the duds in your endless supply of ideas.
- You're likely to get impatient with the 99 percent of people who don't think as fast or as expansively as you do. Watch out for rebuffing those slower thinkers who

might have good ideas or resources to help move your projects along. A front-line "people person" to field questions might be helpful to you.

GROUP #4: GAMBLERS

Where would we be without the Christopher Columbus types like you? How many times were you caught breaking the rules at home or school when you were a kid? An interesting study of successful male entrepreneurs showed that an inordinate number of them were in trouble in school or with the law during their teen years. Your willingness to take risks translates well into exploring new ideas and markets, but could trip you up if you haven't learned to balance your courage with caution.

GOOD NEWS FOR GAMBLERS

- Your fearlessness can take you far. While your competitors hesitate, stopping to check the odds and screw up their courage, you'll already be off and running, beating them to market.
- You've got drive. That will help you keep going when you hit the bumps in the road. Your willingness to work hard for your dreams also greatly enhances your chances of success.
- You'll be terrific when it comes time to present your ideas "out there." Your can-do attitude will attract customers, clients, venture capitalists, potential partners, and others to you.

POTENTIAL PROBLEMS AND ANTIDOTES FOR GAMBLERS

- Watch out for that overdrive gear—it might let you forget the other important parts of your life, which could in turn impair your creativity and judgment.

- Be sure to take enough time to reflect before you rush in to fix things. You might be tempted to ditch a perfectly good idea rather than spend time tinkering with it to make it work.
- Pay attention to what others are telling you (you know, the ones you think are old prunes and naysayers). Your hunches may sometimes be a little too optimistic. For all of the items above, be sure you've given somebody genuine permission to tell you the truth.

GROUP #5: PHILOSOPHERS

You march to the beat of your own drum because you are blessed with a clear sense of what's important to you in life. You probably went on intellectual voyages during boring classes in school, and took refuge from the indignities of growing up in reading or games that stretched your mind. You are probably thoughtful and spiritual, whether you call it that or not. It's also likely that you might need to be pushed to move along a little faster from time to time.

GOOD NEWS FOR PHILOSOPHERS

- The world needs many more people with your wiring—you'll probably live a long and fulfilled life, and have strong relationships to buoy you up in hard times. You're unlikely to get caught up in the overstuffed ego problems that often dog other types of free agents.
- The energy for your undertakings will come from the fact that you really believe in what you're doing. You're respected as a person with integrity and resolve.
- You'll find it easier than other people will to step back and reach thoughtful decisions in hard times. You are generally in touch with your own feelings and values.

POTENTIAL PROBLEMS AND ANTIDOTES FOR PHILOSOPHERS

- You may need to compromise from time to time about the amount of time you think you need for yourself, in order to keep your venture afloat. Some time management training may be helpful.
- Your battery may need recharging now and again, or you may need to get help from high-energy assistants, in order to meet deadlines and finish jobs. You might also need some "practical" advice from time to time, since you seem more at home in the world of thoughts and feelings than in the unforgiving land of contracts, deadlines, and competitors.
- Since making money is often not a prime motivator for you, you probably will need to spend very wisely and be more planful for the long term. A hard-nosed financial advisor is also probably a good idea.

GROUP #6: DESPERADOES

Necessity is, indeed, the mother of invention for many people, and so desperadoes often count on the fact that they really need the money to keep them on track. If you're a desperado, you'll probably be less tempted to waste time or squander opportunities, with the landlord or the credit card company on your heels. If you're a desperado because you weren't able to save enough to have a happy recommencement rather than an impoverished retirement, you'll also probably find that the financial imperatives help you stay on task.

Desperadoes often tell me, after they've figured out how to be successful on their own terms, that they would probably never have pushed themselves to see what they could do had they not had the catalyst of a pressing financial need. Therefore, just as in my book *Toxic Work* I suggested that getting "a little bit sick" could be a wake-up call to change to a less toxic job, so too being "a little bit broke" has more than once lighted a fire under potential free agents who went on to be very successful. Being a desperado can work for you or against you at any point in your process—the trick is to take time enough for both the internal steps and the planning without sacrificing the drive and goal orientation that are usually part of this motivation.

GOOD NEWS FOR DESPERADOES

- Your financial goals will keep you on track when others might slack off. The bottom line realities you're dealing with will help you be more resourceful as well.
- Your individualism can serve you well when it comes to finding a unique niche or brand.
- You're a go-getter—that energy will take you far!

POTENTIAL PROBLEMS AND ANTIDOTES FOR DESPERADOES

- Be sure to ask enough questions about short-term vs. long-term gain in what you're doing. Don't let your immediate need for money cloud your judgment about where to put your energies at any point in time.
- Make certain you've worked through your frustrations about what's been missing for you in the role of "employee," or about why your finances have been problematic—lest you come off as "negative" and turn people off.
- Watch out for your health. Your need for money could push you to miss out on sleep, exercise, relationships, etc. And then where will you be?

So, no matter what your type (or, more likely, your types), you must remember that *there's a cautionary tale accompanying every free agency asset.*

MIXING IT UP

Of course, the *combinations of types* is interesting to consider as well. An *imagineer* who is under-resourced in *gambler* energy, for instance, may find herself being very frustrated by having an abundance of ideas that haven't gotten off the ground because of her aversion to risk. And so she'll have to "install" some gambler confidence in herself, or partner with someone who has it. In reverse, a strong gambler who is not much of an imagineer will need to enlist some creative help to keep up a steady stream of ideas in this volatile economic environment. It's often a lucky combination—a somewhat shy *free spirit* in a *desperado* situation pushes to move beyond his natural reticence to market his work, and so he finds customers for both his web design and photographic skills. The *gambler-rebel-philosopher* combination, meanwhile, worked well for the person willing to quit her job (gambler) as a public interest lawyer (rebel) in order to devote herself to writing full-time (philosopher). You'll meet lots of these "types" in the successful free agent stories in Part Two of the book—see what hints their dilemmas give you about strategies for taking back your own life.

Unfortunately, too many of you doubt your ability to be successful at controlling your own work. After all, that's not what you were taught to expect, particularly if you're 40 or older, if you've been laid off and carry that burden of feeling vulnerable along with you, or if you're a woman having to be a primary breadwinner because of abandonment, divorce or widowhood, or your own choices. Because the stakes seem so high, you might feel naked without the cover of an employment contract and a regular paycheck. (Even though that contract and the paycheck could be null and void in an instant.) Maybe you are also put off by knowing what your own potentially damaging habits are. But *forewarned is forearmed!*

Free agency is not for the faint of heart. You have to be

brutally honest with yourself, and you have to be willing to unearth upsetting information about what's "out there." You also have to be willing to change on a dime. But free agency is a way of life that lets you be who you really are.

It's also critical to understand that designing your own brand of free agency is a seven-step process with both internal and external dimensions. Let Chapter Four show you how to get going—because, as George Eliot promised us, "it's never too late to be what you might have been."

CHAPTER FOUR

Seven Steps to Free Agency

*"The real social revolution of the last 30 years, one
we are still living through, is the switch from a
life that is largely organized for us to a world
in which we are all forced to be in charge
of our own destiny."*

—Charles Handy

We are 600 percent more in debt than we were a decade ago. Our composite credit card debt now exceeds $2.5 trillion. This pattern of financial overextension has compelled many to add a "free agent" component to their work lives. How about you? Perhaps you see no way to live comfortably, pay down your debt, or squeeze out some savings for a reasonable retirement on the salary you're currently able to earn. Or maybe you're one of the millions of workers in their fifties or sixties who have recently learned that your pension and health insurance benefits have somehow been diminished or lost altogether. And so you may be drawn to free agency, either full-time or as a sidecar, because of the opportunity to make more money than you can in the limited and limiting employ of someone else.

For many free agents, however, the issue is not money. It's more emotional and spiritual—something just doesn't feel right about the way they're currently working. If you're one of those people, you're ahead of the game, because you are already tuning in to your own feeling, values, and sense of inner harmony. This is an essential, health-enhancing process which eludes far too many people. Or perhaps you worry about yourself because there seem to be too many parts of you to fit into one job. Are people always telling you to "grow up" or "be sensible and forget all these wild ideas"? Maybe you're wired to be a free agent—someone who needs space to be all of who you are and to change your work over time to fit who you're becoming. Whether your motives for considering free agency are primarily *outer-directed* or *inner-directed,* however, here's the essential news: You must develop both parts of yourself in order to succeed. Highly in-tuitive, spiritually developed people fail at free agency when they pay too little attention to the nitty-gritty aspects of plan-ning, procuring resources, networking, and the like. Great marketers, financiers, and planners fail to achieve lasting suc-cess, meanwhile, when they do not pay enough attention to the interior dimensions of their chosen craft.

Before you try to launch anything, remember to pay at-tention to the seven different steps to successful free agency.

You'll notice that the circle is set up with three phases "be-low the horizon," three above it, and one spanning both. There's a reason for that. Below the horizon is the "Inside Knowing" hemisphere. Traditionally, those elements below the line are the private, more mystical ones, linked to your in-nermost feelings and longings. Here, within the more hidden aspects of yourself, is where your emotional energy and spir-itual power live. And yet, in a materialistic, results-driven, and superficial life, this is the part of you that can be most easily pushed aside. It's hard to make time for introspection in a hurry-up world. For potential free agents, however, neglect-ing those intangibles as you try to imagine and launch your own venture is like starting a trip with no fuel in the tank—you simply won't get where you want to go.

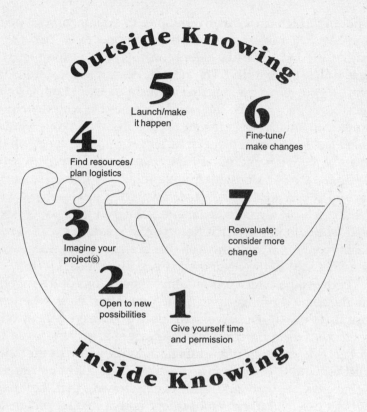

WHERE AND WHEN TO START?

Though it may feel counterintuitive to results-oriented people, starting below the surface, at 6 P.M. (see how #1 is located at the very bottom of the "Inside Knowing" hemisphere), is the best way to begin if you want to have *all of you* represented in your free agency effort. Next you continue clockwise around the circle, touching all seven points, preparing, launching, and fine-tuning until you've come full circle. Then, in time, you'll be ready to begin the process again as you and your ventures evolve.

The first three dimensions are internal because that's where self-knowledge resides. As the venerable Vietnamese

Buddhist Thich Nhat Hanh reminds us, "Enlightenment, peace and joy will not be granted by someone else. The will is within us, and if we dig deeply in the present moment, the water will spring forth." The next three dimensions are external. They're about taking care of business in a planful, strategic, thorough way. The final one, and the one with the largest single amount of space given to it, is the rethinking, reimagining, soul-searching piece. It is, as you might expect, on the cusp of the inner and outer horizons. Here's the rub: *Nothing gets fixed forever.* Constant fine-tuning in response to external factors is essential to the outer level, of course—that's what feedback is. But change is also essential in your inner, spiritual world, to be sure that how you're spending your time is really congruent with the self you are becoming. That's why the final step of the diagram spans both worlds.

Perhaps the "Outside Knowing" dimensions of free agency might come more easily to you. That, after all, is where we live most of our lives. Even people who consider themselves religious, based on church attendance and what goes in the collection plate, are often functioning primarily in the outer, visible world, discounting the yearnings of their interior selves. Or, in some cases, not even allowing that they exist. What's essential to remember here is that neither dimension alone can ensure success. *It's only in the blending and balancing of the two that you get your best results.*

Some of you may already have plunged right into your free agency exploration in the "Outside Knowing" hemisphere and may be wondering why something seems to be missing. If that's the case, you should put your major decisions on hold and move back inside to see where your own thoughts and feelings want to lead you. Resist being buffeted about or deterred—either by the suggestions of others who are guided primarily by their own perceptions and biases or by purely economic considerations. Perhaps you've gotten some of that ill-fitting advice already. There's no doubt that this decade offers you unprecedented opportunity to take charge of your own life. But there's also no doubt that doing it is complicated and fraught with obstacles. The best strategy for making things happen is to go slowly and not shortchange the steps that don't fit so easily with your particular temperament. You can move back and forth above and below the line, blending inner and outer processes as you progress around the circle. Or you may not. But get used to being in motion. *Whatever free agent venture(s) you decide to undertake, you'll need to assess and change continually if you hope to have enduring success.*

Here, then, in more detail, are the seven steps that can take you to success as a free agent.

1. Give yourself time and permission to consider new things

Time—isn't that the most precious commodity? Our "one minute" mindset is on a collision course with how birthing your free agent undertakings really needs to happen. Unless you set aside some time to allow your ideas to take shape, you simply won't be able to do it in a way that fits you emotionally, spiritually, or temperamentally. Brenda Ueland, in her book *If You Want To Write,* observes:

> Inspiration does not come like a bolt, nor is it kinetic energetic striving, but it comes into us slowly and quietly and all the time, though we must regularly and every day give it a little chance to start flowing, prime it with a little solitude and idleness.

When was the last time you took a week, two weeks, or a month away from your work to let what's important for you make its way into your awareness? When's the last time you were really rested even?

Some free agent types find the early steps in the process

harder than others—rebels, imagineers, and gamblers, who often thrive on speed and challenges, find them less to their liking than introspective philosophers.

A somewhat "hyper" young entrepreneur named Jeff (a rebel/gambler combination), for instance, came to see me while he waited for the insurance settlement after his wildly successful retail store was burned out, to talk about what he might want to do next once his legal and financial affairs were in order. "I think I need to take some time to think about things," he said. "Terrific," I responded. "How long?" Expecting him to say something like three to six months, I was shocked when he replied, "Well, at least a week." I can tell you that by the end of a week, this hot-wired guy would have been guaranteed to still be in overdrive, far removed from the introspective state required for step one.

He had said that money was not a big issue for him, so I took the plunge: "This is October. How about thinking about the things we've discussed and doing some research and informational interviews, and then coming back to talk about what might be possible for you sometime after the new year?" He gasped, "I'll probably have gray hair by then." But he agreed.

When he came back in mid-January, his energy was very different. His movements were slower and more fluid. He had designed a plan that included being a part-time financial advisor for start-up ventures and teaching a course in entrepreneurism as an adjunct at a nearby executive MBA program. He had also made a commitment to being with his two small children at least two hours each day, something he could not even have imagined as a busy retailer.

He said, "You know, I almost walked out of your office back in October. I thought you were off in la-la land. I couldn't see how I'd ever be able to be mucking around deciding for that long. But I can see now that it just took time to calm down. It's amazing what a difference that made."

Yes, indeed, *it takes time*. Time away from the "daily-ness" that keeps you putting one foot in front of the other in a re-active state. Time out of doors. Time in a different location altogether. Or even just time carved out from your daily routine. For some, it's a sabbatical of one sort or another. For others, a time of planned unemployment. Only you can decide where you'll find the time to discover what's really important to you, and how you will indeed be able to "do it your way" after all.

Permission is important too. When I spoke with Leighton, a philosopher accountant with a mysterious hankering to turn his woodworking hobby into a sidecar cabinetmaking business, he was a long way from giving himself permission to give up his steady, lucrative job for what his 75-year-old father was calling "that damned fool idea." Even if his father had not been alive and making his opinions so clearly known to his overly obedient son, Leighton would probably have been having trouble. The messages from parents who had lived through the Depression were planted deep in his psyche: *Do what's safe, do what you can count on.*

The only thing that got through to Leighton eventually was my convincing him that *there wasn't anything he could count on in the new economy,* at least as far as having an employer who would keep him on the payroll no matter what. Looking around at what was happening to his friends and cousins in their supposedly "secure" jobs verified that his destiny would have to be of his own making. If that was the case, he decided finally, why not make his destiny something he loved, rather than a pattern his parents had chosen for him long ago.

2. Open to new possibilities

How is this step different from time and permission, you might ask. Well, it is quite different, and many people find it very hard. Deep down, they don't really believe that things can be different, that they can actually create work lives that fit their wishes and needs, rather than vice versa. They are convinced that somehow something will go wrong, and they want to be on the alert just in case. They can't let down their guard enough to free up their own creative juices. These people would make great private investigators, tax accountants, or air traffic controllers, but they drag around a life view that often makes it hard for them to get new ventures airborne.

There are, in fact, two kinds of people—*front-enders* and *back-enders*. Front-enders love the first three stages (and they often count among them imagineers and free spirits). Front-enders love to imagine new things and solve problems. Back-enders, on the other hand, are wired to be cautious and to anticipate problems. Their "best times" are steps four (tending to the plans and details before a launch) and six (fixing whatever needs some fine-tuning). They'll definitely need some help in the early stages, however.

Sometimes opening to the new means shutting down the old—and then seeing what is able to grow in its place. My client Deborah, another long-suffering philosopher, was being assaulted by agonizing headaches, lower back pain, and a pervasive feeling of gloom when she came to talk about her job as a manager of social services programs for at-risk families. There was simply no open space within her to allow for more positive alternatives to manifest themselves. She hadn't a clue about what she'd want to do, other than escape the daily pounding she felt at work.

The only daughter of an alcoholic mother and a work-addicted father, Deborah was in many ways revisiting her childhood by trying to intervene in one dysfunctional family after another, adding more and more work for very little reward. Feeling overwhelmed, out of control, and bereft of emotional resources felt very "normal" to her, as it had all her life. She doubted that she could have any other kind of life. But her body was letting her know that she needed to try. In desperation, Deborah volunteered for a reduction-in-force layoff at her agency, in order to use her separation package and unemployment period to let her mind and body heal. At my suggestion, she sought out other professionals to help her use this opening time well—a wellness trainer, a nutritionist, and a yoga instructor. All of these life-balancing techniques were foreign to her, but she was willing to try anything to feel better.

She also agreed to meet monthly with three other friends who were trying to open up new possibilities for themselves, as a "strategic support group." They gently encouraged each other to imagine being really alive in their work, pushing each other to consider ideas they would once have thought outrageous. With time, a vision slowly came to life inside Deborah, which she tested out and developed by talking first to her group and then to formerly dubious friends, family, and colleagues. Six months later, Deborah was ready to start in earnest planning for her own consulting-and-training practice working with schools and nonprofits around conflict resolution and mediation. A year later, she was launched. Finally, the exhausted "rescuer" within her had been replaced by a self-sufficient grown-up. But none of this would have happened without her period of recuperation.

Because the *opening up* step is very subtle, some people miss the need for it altogether. This step requires that you anticipate (or get some help identifying) your own *internal roadblocks*, which by their very nature resist being discovered and invited out into the open. If you're a back-ender who is drawn naturally more to what can go wrong than to the possibilities in situations, then opening to new ideas could be a challenge for you—you'll very likely shoot down your own ideas before they get off the ground. If you've organized your life around what's good for others rather than what you really want, that's trouble too. And if you're afraid to loosen your grip on the little security you think you have, then you're also compromising your eventual success, because you're not making any space for new ideas to sprout.

So gather up your courage and ask three people *how ready you seem,* on a scale of one to ten, *to explore new possibilities for yourself.* If your numbers come back at seven or below, you've got some things to think and talk about.

3. Imagine your project(s)

For some of you, especially imagineers, imagining is easy—you do it all the time, even when you're supposed to be taking care of today's business. For others, particularly those who are good at organizing and at following through on specific tasks and assignments, it's often terribly anxiety-producing, because it requires you to move outside the realm of what's known, measurable, and predictable. But *imagine you must,* if you want to work more freely, either part-time or full-time, at something that has real meaning for you. How about you—does it come naturally or not? I often "prescribe" a period of confusion, urging clients not to try to nail it all down too soon, in order to give themselves time to play with enough possibilities. The free-agents-in-training who receive this prescription are seldom pleased to get it at first—but most are eventually glad they did.

Here are some of the questions I pose to people who are trying to peer inside their own underutilized imaginations, to see what ventures or opportunities might bring more "juice" to their lives. See if any of them can get you wondering a little. As you respond to each question, you might want to jot down the key ideas that come to you. (See the "Imagination Booster" in Part Three.)

- Suppose I gave you $1,000 to spend at your favorite bookstore this afternoon. What kinds of books would you buy? Why? What do your choices tell you about interests and values of yours that might be relevant to different career options for you in the future?

- Think back over the past several months. When have you been jealous or envious of others? Of whom? For what reasons? If you could have what they have, what would that do for you?
- Remember what you liked to do in the third, fourth, fifth, or sixth grade and in junior high school. What were you best at then? How did that feel? Can you imagine turning something related to those activities into a part-time or full-time activity now?
- With whom would you like most to change places for a week? Why? What about their lives is most appealing to you?
- What's the most fun you have in your life now? Is there anything related to those times or activities that could be developed into something you could get paid for?
- I've just given you a check for $100,000 to give away to one or more charities. To whom would you make your gift(s) and why? Do you see any clues there about what's important to you—and hence about how you might put your passions to work?
- Name three of your personal heroes or heroines. What about the life or achievements of each one has special meaning for you? What hints about the meaning and experiences you're seeking in your work do the lives of these special people give you?
- If you were suddenly free (or if you are free) to make a new personal partnership, what kind of person would you choose? Why? What qualities would you want that person to help bring into your life? What's the possibility that you could find some of those things *for yourself* by changing how you do your work?

Now look over the ideas you jotted down—what do you see in your responses? If you just pretend you're your own counselor, or if you and somebody else ask each other these questions, or if you take your responses to your own counselor or coach, you'll be on your way to discovering what might *put more passion in your life.* As Simone Weil warns, "Nothing in the world can make up for the lack of joy in one's work." Yet another way to prime the pump is to ask five or ten people who know you well the following question: *Suppose I were to quit the work I'm doing tomorrow. You know my talents and interests, and you know the kinds of services or products the world needs now. If money were no object, what kind of free agent venture or work would you see me getting involved in?* Or better yet, raise this question about *everybody* at your next party or cookout, and see how many little firecrackers of possibility you can set off. You don't have to have it all figured out now. You just have to be able to imagine some ideas, and then move into a period of exploring how they might work. I've seen some people get a new venture pulled together in three months, while others have taken nine or ten years to figure it out. Either speed is fine: Your "career metabolism" is unique to you.

You'll also be glad if you keep a "career log" during this imagining time—and even after as you fine-tune your ideas. The shelf life of most ideas is about one month (most of us will forget 90 percent of our thoughts within 30 days), so you'll want to "harvest" all of your ideas and preserve them for present or future consideration. An insight is a terrible thing to waste.

4. Find the resources you'll need and plan the logistics

In order to make a success of whatever you're planning, you're going to need three quite different kinds of expertise:

1. Business or professional information
2. Business or professional acumen
3. Personal competence—or "emotional intelligence"

The easiest one of the three is *information*—it's everywhere, we're drowning in it. It's sometimes a challenge to figure out the quality and know whom to believe—and that's where *acumen* comes in. If you've got some workplace experience to your credit and have learned from the collisions you've survived, then you may be well enough endowed with this second quality. But if you're new to the workplace or a bit challenged in this area, chances are you'll need to hire or contract with people who have it, or get lots of advice from business advisors like the kind folks from SCORE (Service Corps of Retired Executives). If you're not in business, but rather in the arts or a profession, you're still going to need lots of practical advice, from one of your professional organizations, books, and web sites.

Whether you're *starting a new business or service* or *making art,* here are some people you'll very likely need to know:

- Bankers and/or venture capitalists
- Marketers
- Advertising outlets
- Publicists
- Agents
- Legal advisors
- Accountants and bookkeepers
- Computer service people and/or tutors
- "Business to business" vendors of services and products
- Web site designers/managers
- Strategic support groups of colleagues with expertise in your field
- Professional coaches or paid supervisors
- "Support" staffers willing to work flexibly at affordable rates

Don't try to get where you're going without sufficient access to whatever external resources fit your venture.

Of course, organization counts too. Are you a planner or a

seat-of-the-pants type? If you're a planner, you'll love this section, because it says what you already know, and that makes you feel good. (Also, this is the opposite of that imagination thing from step three that you probably found to be a little problematic.) If you're hooked on spontaneity, you're not going to like this section. But you really need it. *Whatever you're going to do will take a plan.* And it needs to be a plan on paper. Too simplistic, you say? I don't think so. If you've borrowed money from a bank to fund a venture, you have had a plan—because the nice man or woman at the bank wouldn't have been so nice had you not come up with the requisite business and marketing plan.

But you can't imagine how many folks trying to launch something on a shoestring, away from the watchful eye of a lender, have not bothered to write it down, check out the details with some knowledgeable people, use the calculator, and see if it was going to work. That ostrich planning happens all the time. When it does, great ideas fail, which is in turn a tremendous waste of your inner resources. So figure out how long you think you'll need to find the information to write a thorough plan—and then double it. Whether you do it yourself or end up hiring someone to create it, don't shortchange this part of the process, whatever you do!

Probably the most important resource you'll need, and the one that seems to trip up eager free agents most frequently, is *personal competence.* Psychologist Dan Goleman has written a great deal about EQ (emotional intelligence) and its role in workplace success. He and other EQ experts have identified more than 25 personal characteristics that seem to correlate with success, as a person and as a worker. It's estimated that up to 95 percent of career success is determined by how well endowed we are with these qualities, and that figure certainly has been borne out in my work as a coach and counselor. The five that I believe are *most basic to succeeding as a free agent* are the following:

1. Realistic self-appraisal, underscored by a desire to improve constantly and confidence that you'll be able to get where you want to go
2. Adaptability and flexibility—being able to confront problems and land on your feet, again and again
3. Optimism—a positive outlook on the world
4. Self-control and consistent follow-through
5. Initiative and drive

An essential assessment for you to undertake, then, in the resource finding and planning of step four is getting a dead-honest analysis of where you stand on these five kinds of *personal competence.*

You'll have a chance in the "Have You Checked Your EQ Yet?" story to see the Personal Competencies Grid that Doug used to check out his state of free agency readiness. That might give you a sense of where you are in your own development of these five elements of personal mastery for free agents. (See also the "EQ Checklist" in Part Three.)

5. Launch/Make it happen

Gamblers are probably in the best shape in step five, but many of you probably don't share their bravado. It's at this point that many folks, particularly shy or introspective ones, have to take a trip back inside to ask themselves some hard questions about whether they really want to do this thing they've dreamed up. That's a fine and appropriate detour. Eventually, however, if you decide to continue, it *will be time* to jump, lead, take off, and be visible to all the world. (Or at least it will seem that way.) After the launch, you'll need to keep your roster of people and resources at hand, calling on them in advance of trouble whenever you can.

Be aware that pride can be a huge enemy of success at this point. I can still see the shameful look on free spirit Lucas's face when his partner Matthew sent him to see me about his writer's block. He had a $40,000 contract to complete a book on gay male relationships, and the clock was ticking. He had taken a six-month sabbatical from his practice as a psychologist to complete the first draft of the book, but he hadn't been able to write for more than a month. With each passing day he had become more panicked and less functional.

And so I asked, "What do the people in your writers group have to say about where you're stuck in the manuscript?" He didn't have one.

"What about your friends to whom you've shown what you've written so far?" He had been too shy to show his work to anyone. Even his partner Matthew had only seen the proposal.

"If I can't do it myself, then I don't want to do it," he protested. This was very strange behavior for a psychologist, even a young one, but it's so easy to forget what you know when the pressure to produce moves in on you.

I pointed out to Lucas that he had the guts of one chapter for his book right here in our interaction: *the importance of showing your vulnerability as an essential part of relationships.* Fortunately, he didn't take too long to see that his proud Lone Ranger stance was surely sinking his project. He agreed to have a consultation with a writing therapist in the area who had worked for years with doctoral candidates. He also agreed to let Matthew read what he had so far over the weekend, and to find at least two other people to form an impromptu writing group, for help with both the content and the style of his project. The good news is that he finished the book and it sold well. The best news is that he learned a lot about finding and using resources.

Another serious question when you're about to launch something is money. Just as you check for your wallet, traveler's checks, and credit cards when you're pulling out of the driveway, now's the time to check on your *money habits.* If you're too cautious with money, you can get tripped up by missing opportunities to invest in good ideas or by being too hesitant to spend enough to get the visibility you need. "It takes money to make money" is surely true—even more so in the new information economy.

Most of you, however, will probably err on the *other side* of the open vs. closed wallet issue. Not a small amount of personal debt has been brought about by the expenses of free agents getting launched. But there's "good debt" (the kind that will lead to increased income) and "bad debt" (the kind that comes from impulse shopping, keeping up appearances, and generally anesthetizing yourself against the stresses and dissatisfactions in your life).

Free agents can't afford any more bad debt. So, before you take off, be sure that your "regular" spending has been whittled to the minimum. Make a list of all your monthly expenses—both professional and personal—and then start asking around about what others in your life spend in these areas. You might be in for a shock! If you find that your expenses are higher than other people's, you might be wise to delay your launch until you've found a way to pound the fat out of your budget. Why, you say?

It's easy. Most debt has been undertaken with an "employee" mindset, i.e., "x amount of salary or wages equals the ability to pay this off." Well, we've already said that free agency is an economic roller coaster of great months and terrible months. As you launch, you can't afford to be carrying any bills that aren't absolutely necessary to your survival. Give your venture a year and *then* think about spending more money on yourself. For now, however, *whatever you don't owe or spend* will give you many more *degrees of freedom* for getting your venture launched.

The reasons for ventures stalling, conking out, or never getting off the ground are more numerous than the number of potential free agents out there trying to make them happen. But here are a few that show up regularly, both for me and my counseling and coaching clients. See if any of them sound familiar to you and, if they do, try some of the antidotes below:

- Lack of focus. *Your brain chatter is making it hard to prioritize and bring a single-minded, laser intensity to any one project.* It's easier to start something new when you've learned to quiet your noisy brain with some kind of meditative practice that works for you. For more physical types, activities like yoga, walking, or running are often helpful, particularly if you set yourself the task of getting more focused as you begin the activity.

- Fear. *You're standing up there on the diving board, terrified to jump.* "Instructions" vary tremendously from teacher to teacher on this one—some folks are adamant about a "tough love" approach, while others are gentler. I favor a middle-of-the-road strategy: setting a realistic time frame for what you want to accomplish, and then enlisting the support of a trusted friend, family member, coach, or counselor to hold you to it. Often, just saying out loud that you're afraid and asking for help does the trick.

- Procrastination. *You just can't get organized enough to have all the pieces in place.* This is first cousin to fear, of course. The "helpful but directive coach" approach works here too. Sometimes the problem is so long-standing, however, that you'll want a professional organizer to come and help you clear out your work space enough to see clearly what the obstacles are. If the clutter is internal as well as external, as it so often is, a counselor or coach may well be necessary.

- Shyness. *You're too inhibited to ask for the help you're definitely going to need.* This one is a killer. You simply can't make great things happen all by yourself. Period. If this is what's holding you back, find a counselor or

one person you think you can trust, and talk it out with
that person.

- Lack of conviction. *You doubt at some level that it can
really work.* You'll need to go inside again and double-
check the *permission* thing. You might also want to
share your plan with somebody who knows about
these things to be sure it's really a viable one. Maybe
this is just self-doubt, but it could be your good judgment talking—don't be afraid to scuttle a plan if your
doubts turn out to be realistic. Remember Emerson's
admonition that "a foolish consistency is the hobgoblin
of little minds." Perhaps you've unearthed a real problem and should listen to yourself.

- Family disapproval. *You're finding out that family negativity cancels out your enthusiasm pretty quickly.* Just
remember that it's a rare family that's really able to
move beyond their own individual preferences and biases to evaluate objectively the ventures or moves you
might be considering. Here's another thing to remember about families. Some of them are addicted to worry,
largely because they have the mistaken impression that
a good way to prove you love somebody is to worry
about them.

Cognitive psychologists will tell you, of course, that
being "worried about" by somebody actually under-
mines your confidence, because you begin to wonder
whether there's some truth to the concern. So the worrier is in reality contributing to the very situation he or
she is supposedly trying to prevent. But try to tell your
mother, your uncle, or your grandmother that. So, if you
really want to do it, *just do it.* Once it's successful,
they'll all come around and forget how much they
doubted you. And if they don't, why let others' negativity limit your own possibilities? If the worrier is a
spouse or partner, that's a different story. In that case,

you're going to need to do some conflict resolution, on your own or with a counselor trained in "family systems." Either way, the disapproval and concern should be confronted and worked through.

- Time management. *You have a hard time knowing how long things really take and how to prioritize conflicting demands.* You'd better get this one fixed now, through some combination of a good system and some coaching. If it's a problem as you're launching, it's sure to take an even bigger bite as you get more successful, and busier.

- Lack of back-up. *You're not prepared for things to go wrong.* Pretend there's a huge storm coming. You're going to need some cushions—in terms of cash or credit, labor, materials, problem-solving, and creative ideas. Have them lined up in advance, so that you won't need to go searching for them frantically when you need them—because you're definitely going to have challenges.

6. Fine-tune and make changes

Congratulations—you've planned and planned and you've anticipated every detail and *you've launched your venture,* large or small. But count on the fact that at least several things won't be right. Hopefully, the very first thing you planned for was a *feedback system,* a way to test out how things are going. If you're in a business, sales (and then profit, hopefully) will be the ultimate feedback. But you'd also better plan on building in more immediate ways to collect information from customers and potential customers. Some folks are so afraid of failing that they can't bring themselves to ask how their customers or clients are reacting to what they're offering. Use customer feedback cards, client reaction forms, focus groups, polls and surveys, e-mail options or counters on various segments of your web site—whatever it takes—to find out how people are responding (or not responding) to what you're putting out there. And then do something about what you discover, sooner rather than later.

Sometimes, the fine-tuning will need to come because of what you find out about *yourself* rather than about your customers, clients, readers, or patients. You might find out that five days at your massage practice is too many, and that you could see the same number of people in four long days, have a fifth day to recuperate, and do better work. You might find out that you're a great artist but a lousy marketer, and that you need to hire someone to do your publicity and marketing. Perhaps you'll find out that the product you like best in your new line of crafts has zero customer appeal, and so you'll sell off what you have at a reduced cost and replace it with something else. One thing is for sure—something about what you're doing will need fine-tuning, and, eventually, a major change.

You steeled yourself to criticism so that you could gather client feedback, you've made some modifications, and now it's finally working. Why would you need to change anything else? *Because that's the way the world of free agency works.* As futurist Rowan Gibson observed, "No one can drive to the future on cruise control." If you're in business you'll have no choice but to vary your product mix and/or upgrade your services—well before anybody complains about them. If you're an artist, you may well need to try a new medium or experiment with different ways to make your work visible. If you're developing a sidecar venture, you may need to negotiate a different contract with your employer, so as to have enough time to tend whatever it is you're trying to grow. Our friend Lucas, for instance, needed to renegotiate his writing contract to get more time from his publisher when his sabbatical was almost up. Other people also renegotiated one way or another. Derek found a way to work four long days as a designer and have Fridays "off" to teach art classes. Marian moved from public school teaching to a private school, where the vacations are longer and the days shorter, in order to have time for getting her social work degree part-time. Ginger, meanwhile, worked out a way to go part-time at her bank teller job in order to give more time to her growing network marketing business.

You may even decide to change ventures altogether, based on what the market is doing or what internal changes you're experiencing. The possible variations on the theme are too lengthy to list, even in a much longer book. *Just don't give up*—and know that there's no way to escape the need to keep on modifying your products or your practice. For, as Will Rogers reminded us, "When you're through changing, you're all through."

7. Reevaluate and consider more change

You mean I have to do *more introspection?* And consider *more change?* Some self-aware people move back and forth between their inner and outer hemispheres all the time. But even for those who don't do that easily, it will inevitably be time to go back inside to your own dreams, and then step outside to test the viability of what you've found. In the long run, any changes or decisions you try to make without going "inside" to test out what your heart is telling you will be shallow and ill-fitting. On the other hand, trying to take your dreams to market without external testing also guarantees failure. And you have to keep on doing them both, again and again.

Here's an example of a need to fine-tune that took one free agent by surprise. Imagineer/philosopher Jim, who had previously been a successful hospital administrator but found very little meaning in his work, had made a courageous leap into health care advocacy, advising individuals and families about the medical resources and options available to them. Because the need for ethical, objective advice was great and he lived in an affluent area, his practice flourished. He also enjoyed speaking at conferences, consulting to various groups, and writing for his web site and various magazines. It was a tremendous improvement for Jim, who had been very relieved to trade the maximal-profit "company man" aspects of health care for more humanitarian concerns. So he was baffled when, after a year or so in his new role, he started missing being part of a team. Though he didn't want to go back to working in a hospital, he did want the camaraderie of problem-solving with others. "What's wrong with me?" he asked exasperatedly. "Will I never be satisfied?"

"Of course you will, for a while," I answered. "But then it will be time to change in some major way again. So get used to it. Companies make new and improved models and products all the time. Why shouldn't free agent professionals be changing too?

"What pieces of your old job are you missing most?" I asked. "And how could you recreate just those parts in what you're doing now?"

And so Jim figured out that his need for having people around him could be served by pulling together a group of colleagues in various medical and allied health specialties as a loose-knit health and mental health collaborative. They met twice a month for a long dinner meeting, sharing concerns and materials. There they discussed strategies for returning back into their respective professions some of the meaning that had brought them into health care. In the end, they were good for each other, and functioned as a strong voice in local health care reform. And Jim had met his need for colleagues without going back to work in a hospital and feeling "owned" again.

Susan, the free spirit, also needed to consider both inside and outside concerns in her seventh step. She was in her eighth year of a financially successful practice as a massage therapist and movement teacher, when she came back to tell me that "our solution" wasn't working anymore. "We must have made some miscalculations," she opined.

"You aren't the same person you were ten years ago," I observed. "So why would you expect that all of the old plan would still fit?"

Susan's dilemma was that she had taken some film courses, and had decided that she wanted to be a filmmaker. But how could she travel the world to make films and abandon her clients and students? How could she make a living? I suggested to Susan that she had fallen into the "either/or" trap of forgetting that she could take the best of one career idea and marry it to parts of the other in whatever pattern fit her best.

So many people get tripped up here, thinking that loving animals means going to vet school; that being good at instructing means being imprisoned in a seventh-grade classroom; that liking to draw means starving in a sparsely furnished garret. *Hardly*. Passions can be added to careers like accessories. Once Susan figured out during this reevaluation interlude that she didn't need to trade in her holistic health practice to be a Hollywood camp follower, she was able to turn her new love of filmmaking and her abiding interest in Jewish religious practices into another activity for her "career collage." With several like-minded friends from her synagogue, she began devoting one evening a week to planning for a teaching video about movement and spirituality. Within six months, her group had produced a 30-minute film, which they then used as the centerpiece for day-long spiritual intensives that they offered, first in their own place of worship, and then for regional conferences. An emerging passion that at first had seemed to be on a collision course with Susan's holistic free agency practice actually turned out to enrich and deepen it.

WHAT IS MORE IMPORTANT—
INNER OR OUTER?

Neither one. I know this firsthand. Some of my ideas have failed because there just wasn't enough real spiritual purpose behind them. I have nearly a foot of dusty drafts of book and program proposals in my attic to prove that one. Other projects have flopped because I didn't calculate the nitty-gritty details carefully enough. The same is true with the many thousands of clients I've helped "start a little something" in their lives. Ideally, you'd start your venture from an inner sense of conviction and purpose and grow your idea from there. But some people have started from purely practical perspectives and then later on course-corrected to imbue their ventures or undertakings with more meaning. Eventually, you'll have to get into your inner space if you want to be truly happy and fulfilled with what you've started. And of course the external concerns, the taking-care-of-business factors, are essential as well.

Hopefully the next twenty-two stories will speak to some of your questions or doubts about whether free agency could work for you, and help you to do both the outer and inner work to succeed. There is nothing in the world more powerful than making your living doing what you believe in and choreographing a life that is consistent not only with your skills, relationships, values, and temperament, but with your own unique rhythm as well, either on your own or in an organization. That's what *Free to Succeed* asks you to believe and act on at the most propitious time. You must ask yourself the hard questions in all seven steps of the free agency cycle and act on your answers in good faith, no matter how hard they are to hear. Then you will move ever closer to knowing what Mahatma Gandhi meant when he said, "I am committed to truth—not consistency."

You are very likely leading an incredibly busy and fragmented life in this volatile new free agent economy, whether you're currently functioning as a free agent or not. Taking time to reread a book is a luxury few of you have, I would imagine. Also, people seem to learn and remember best through stories. The ones that follow in Part Two will give you easy access to the *six free agent "styles"* and the *seven essential "steps"* whenever you need them, to remind yourself about how to stay on track—without starting the book all over again.

Staying focused on your goals and keeping your confidence high are two necessary components of being successful on your own terms. These stories will help you be "re-infected" with contagious enthusiasm whenever you need it, wherever you are in the free agency process. You'll probably find yourself and people you know in one or more of the next twenty-two stories in Part Two. Take them along as mentors on your own journey to designing and living the life you want to lead.

22 STORIES FOR FREE AGENTS

"Idealists . . . foolish enough to throw caution to the winds . . . have advanced mankind and have enriched the world."

—Emma Goldman

STEP ONE

---------------------------------------→

Give Yourself Time
and Permission

"Let me listen to me, and not to them."

—Gertrude Stein

Even when your work life is boring, unsettling, or even painful for one reason or another, it's often not easy to take the *time* you need to consider your options carefully—or to grant yourself *permission* to break out of whatever constraints are at work for you. Somehow it's easier to "keep on keeping on" in a half-alive state than to make the decision to do what you need to do for yourself.

The stories that follow will help you to understand the need to take this time out, with examples of how other potential free agents have broken through their own limitations. See, for instance, how imagineer Todd wrestles with the business offer his brother-in-law has made him, and how 74-year-old Martha, a blend of free spirit and rebel, lets herself move beyond the ageist assumptions of her friends and family.

- **Empty Raincoats**
- **Ghosts**
- **Maybe I'm Too Old For This**

Empty Raincoats

*"It seems as if we're in danger of destroying our
souls . . . We're all becoming empty raincoats,
shadows, silhouettes of ourselves. And we're
doing it to ourselves . . . because we're too
lazy to take on the responsibility of
finding out who we are."*

—Charles Handy

When British economist and philosopher Charles Handy returned to England after a visit to Minneapolis, where he encountered a sculpture of an empty raincoat, he couldn't get it out of his mind. And so that image found its way into his book *The Empty Raincoat: Making Sense of the Future.* That image of vacancy and depletion is a fitting one to launch our consideration of the first step, *Give yourself time and permission to consider new things.* Nobody ever starts thinking about change because things are going along swimmingly—the catalysts are almost always things going wrong or a feeling that something important is missing.

Here's where *taking time* matters. People have often been keeping themselves from knowing they're empty by staying busy. They purposely leave precious little time for noticing the feelings that signal the need for serious changes. Over time, however, the cavity enlarges. Then the empty raincoats (or suits) experience depression, anxiety, and an assortment of physical symptoms. If the signals are ignored, they just get stronger until, finally, there is no choice but to pay attention.

But here's the good news. In every case where I've been able to persuade someone to *take some time to think about what he or she really wants more of,* that person has been able to make a space for buried emotions and desires to emerge, and somehow to create a plan that really works.

So how do you get the time you need to go beneath the surface of your anesthetized life, to know what you're really feeling, thinking, and longing for? Here are some different approaches that people have found helpful.

- Setting aside time to go away, alone or with a special friend or partner, to classes, conferences, sweat lodges, or retreat centers of various kinds.
- Taking meditative time each day, so that you compensate for the shortness of the time with the promise of repetition—making that alone time an essential part of each day.
- Taking long walks on a regular basis, tape recorder in hand, recording your thoughts about things you haven't given yourself time to consider lately.
- Asking someone who knows you really well (and is not afraid to tell you the truth) on a scale of 1 to 10 just how "full" and contented you seem. This is most effective when you promise yourself in advance that for every point less than ten in your score you'll take off two days from work to indulge in quiet, contemplative time.
- Driving to the closest body of water, mountain, or wooded area early one morning and staying there until the end of the day, walking, catching a few winks, picnicking by yourself, just thinking about whatever comes to mind. Nothing, absolutely nothing, gets you *into your own interiors* better than spending time alone in nature.
- Finding an inexpensive motel and going there alone for the weekend, with nothing but some classical music or meditation tapes and writing materials. And don't turn on the television or radio—it's your interior reality, not the external circus, you're needing to connect with.
- Calling a friend who's known you forever, and asking him or her for the gift of one day's time alone with you, someplace out of the hubbub of dailiness.

- Packing up a sketch pad and pencil, pen or paints, going someplace to spend the day alone putting some representation of what you're feeling (and not feeling) onto paper.

And once you're there in that quiet space, with time to get inside yourself, how do you get to the level of self-awareness and acceptance that you're seeking? Our most important notions, says author Brenda Ueland, "slip into our souls some other day when we are doing nothing." Self-acceptance is important here: You have to be willing to accept whatever comes up as okay, not open to censure or ridicule by your rational, practical, or sophisticated self.

The possible list of questions to ponder is infinite, obviously. Here are a few I've posed over the years. Answer a few, and then add your own. (See the "My Own Alone Time" exercise in Part Three.)

- When is the last time I was alone? What feelings came up for me then? What do I think (or fear) might come up now?
- What could I imagine doing if I didn't have to go to work for a year? Why am I not doing some of those things now?
- When I was a little child, what comforts do I remember loving? How could I create some of those comforts for myself now?
- What is my hurrying up about now? What's happening inside me that I don't want to face? And whose approval am I trying to earn?
- Whom would I disappoint if I slowed down? What other terrible things do I fear might happen?
- I'm so tired—what am I tired of?
- What's missing for me? Where did the body and spirit inside my raincoat go? What could I do to get them back?

First *time,* then *permission*—that's generally how step one goes. As educator Parker Palmer pointed out, "Vocation does not mean a goal that I pursue. It means a calling that I hear." Listening for the "vocation" that can give you back your life will require time out, time away, quiet time. Don't try to short-change that process, no matter how impractical or frustrating it may seem at the beginning.

Ghosts

*"You may be disappointed if you fail, but you are
doomed if you don't try."*

—Beverly Sills

Sometimes free agency is roadblocked because not enough
time has been taken. And sometimes it's a *permission* problem. Todd, the 38-year-old marketing executive on the other
end of the phone line, was distraught, to say the least. "My
brother-in-law, who has offered me a partnership in an internet company he's buying, has suggested I call you, to talk
about whether to take his offer," he began. "But I have to
warn you, I'm really feeling stuck. I just can't seem to decide
whether this is a good move for me or not."

And therein began a multiweek epic of many hours of
telephone calls back and forth from Philadelphia to Massachusetts, as this capable guy, who had an endless supply of
creative ideas and was quite able to make effective marketing decisions at the telecommunications firm where he
worked, came apart at the seams about the personal decision
he was facing. The first hours were spent discussing the logical details—which of his several alternatives would work
best for his long-range vs. short-range goals and what he
might expect as daily fare in each of the two options he was
considering, for instance. The discussions were lively and
punctuated by several short "homework" assignments. But
alas, they produced no decision. Time was running out. In
terms of the six free agency "types," it was clear that Todd
was high in *imagineer* but near empty on *gambler*.

And so very close to the end of the time he had been
given to decide, it was clear that this supposedly strategic discussion was being hijacked by emotional, "internal" issues.
"Tell me what your parents would say to you about this

choice," I asked finally. Todd was silent. Then slowly he began to talk about his family.

His mother, a powerful woman with whom he had had a very close relationship, was dead. Physically, at least. While she was alive, however, she had been very active in planning her son's life. She had, in fact, strongly influenced most of his personal decisions.

"And what would Dad have to say? What kinds of decisions did he make in his life?"

"Well, I imagine he'd tell me to stay put. He took a major chance on a big job once when I was just a kid and the company folded. He was never able to find a decent position after that. I remember him saying over and over that it's important not to make mistakes like that."

Todd was beginning to take in the enormity of what his family history was saying to him in this moment of decision-making.

Finally, I spoke. "So you're being held hostage here by ghosts—first, by your dead mother, whom you're afraid you'll disappoint by making the 'wrong' (i.e., different from hers) choice. And by the failures of your father, whose life has been an unspoken but constant lesson for you about not taking risks."

Ghosts, they're everywhere. And they are particularly problematic for people who grew up in the shadow of the "company man" and predictable career ladder mythology, but who are now wrestling with the challenges of a volatile, risk-driven economy. Sally Kempton reminds us that "it's hard to fight an enemy who has outposts in your head." But if you're thinking about moving beyond the stuck places of other people's experiences, to give yourself *permission* to dream free agent economy dreams, that's exactly what you'll need to do.

Here's an assignment to help you have a look at some of your own ghosts. Think of a person with whom you have an open and trusting relationship—someone you can count on to listen, with both objectivity and compassion, to the information I'm going to ask you to share. Or, you could do it with several people, as they do in Quaker "Clearness Committee" meetings. This is a tradition that brings together a small group of friends to help someone clarify her or his thinking about a problem or an impending decision. In that group, where wise and gentle acceptance is assured, no matter what you say, it's usually possible to experience your own blind spots and stuck places. (See the "Clearness Committee" exercise in Part Three.)

Once you have an individual listener or a group selected, here are the questions for you to answer. And of course you'll have your own to add to this list.

1. In your life, to whom have you looked for help in making major decisions? What would that person (or persons) say to you now about the decision you're making?
2. What examples of risks taken and not taken have you seen, particularly as a child or young person, in the lives of people close to you?
3. What examples of successful risks taken can you remember from the stories told by your family and extended family/friends?
4. What did those successful people do to succeed? Be as concrete as you can with this one.
5. Now go back to the failures—what behaviors, attitudes, or skill deficits seem to you to account for the failures of people close to you who didn't achieve their goals? Again, be concrete. What do you see now that they might have done differently?
6. What is it that you're really looking for? And if you got that, what would it do for you?
7. How likely is it that each of the choices you're considering now could give you what you want?

Imagine that you're at a table with a successful person and an unsuccessful person from your family's cast of characters. Let's "listen in" as you ask them to debate with each other as to whether you should take the risk you're imagining. I think you'll be amazed at the clarity of thought that can come from opening the closet doors and inviting the ghosts to come out and converse, with you and with each other.

That imaginary family debate was helpful for Todd. As we talked, he "invited" his uncle Mort, his father's older brother who had been dead for nearly ten years, to "converse" with him about the family messages. Some liberating details emerged. By asking Todd to dig deep into splinters of old memories, I helped him to see that he was not at all like his father—who had tried to charm his way through life and never was willing to work hard enough to be successful. Todd was shocked, but grateful for this different lens being applied to his "ghosts."

Finally, Todd did decide to put his great *imagineering* capabilities and marketing skills to work in the new family business shortly thereafter. He also made a pact with himself to watch and learn from his two new partners, one a *gambler* and one a *free spirit/desperado* combination. Finally, he also agreed to begin short-term cognitive behavioral therapy, to make sure those ghosts didn't crawl back inside and try to take up residence again. Todd had come to believe Anaïs Nin's admonition that "life shrinks or expands in direct proportion to one's courage," and he wasn't taking any chances.

Maybe I'm Too Old for This

"People don't grow old. When they stop growing,
they become old."

—Deepak Chopra

As I welcomed Martha, the spirited, white-haired, 74-year-old Smith alumna into my office, I thought she looked a little bit uncomfortable. After several minutes of establishing a connection, she started right in on her story. "I'm here because I'm just finishing my doctorate in future studies at the university, and I don't know what to do with it."

"Tell me more," I urged her. She spoke of having been a successful real estate agent for many years, and of retiring eight years earlier when her husband retired. They had plans to travel and do all the things they hadn't done while they were both working so hard. But he had died suddenly, just three years into their retirement, and she had been left to make sense of her life alone. Going back to real estate seemed a little impractical and somewhat regressive, and so, quite characteristically, Martha, a blend of *free spirit* and *rebel,* had decided on a big challenge. She enrolled in a doctoral program at the university where she had completed a master's degree thirty-five years earlier.

"And now," she said, "here I am. Some days I feel ready to go out and really accomplish something important. But on the other days, I think to myself, 'Oh, act your age, will you? Be sensible, what are you doing with these big ideas?'"

"What kinds of big ideas?" I inquired eagerly.

"Oh, I don't know—just things like getting more senior citizens to go to college, organizing seniors to be more involved in working with children and teens. I've also thought of starting feminist book groups for women over 60, because the younger women I've met in my classes just don't seem to understand either the struggles or the victories we've had, and that's frustrating."

"Those ideas all seem wonderful, and quite possible. So let's look more closely at this standoff you're experiencing. Do you think it's about your lack of ability or of opportunity, or about the negativity you're osmosing from the environment?"

She knew the answer, of course. As we talked, I reminded her of the fact that Grandma Moses had taken up needlework at age 67 when her husband died, then switched to painting at age 78 because of her arthritis; she died at 101 just after completing her last painting, called *Rainbow*. I reminded her also of Libba Cotton who had written her song, "Freight Train" (a Peter, Paul and Mary hit), at age 11, but didn't perform it herself until age 60. The oldest person ever to win a Grammy, she died at 95 in her hometown of Syracuse. Then we talked of the Older Women's League founded by Tish Summer and Laurie Shields. Their theme: "Organize, don't agonize."

We also talked about the 100-year-old Ayurvedic seer Adi Shankara's wry observation that the only reason people grow old and die is because they see other people doing it. Psychologist Ellen Langer confirmed that to some degree in her research with older people in a nursing home. She asked her subjects about their earliest memories of their grandparents. She heard the full spectrum of scenarios, everything from children being afraid of decrepit or cantankerous old people to children reveling in contacts with grandparents who were lively, generous, and funny. Then Langer examined the health records of the storytellers. Just as she expected, she found that those older people with the most positive attitudes and the best health were the ones whose grandparents had modeled for them a more joyous and healthy way to be old. The sickest, most negative ones had somehow been "imprinted" with the notion that getting old means being sick or helpless.

Indeed, Martha remembered her grandfather as someone who worked until he was 78 and stayed involved with the community into his nineties. Memories of him had encouraged her to enroll at the university four years earlier. *But it was sometimes hard to hold onto that image.* That was the checkmate playing itself out for Martha—should she expect to use her degree with gusto, or was she fighting a losing battle as so many around her seemed to be saying?

When she left that first session, she had her homework in hand:

- Get her business cards listing herself as a consultant
- Contact Smith alumnae in the area who were working in interesting organizations to talk about their work and where they saw activities for seniors being developed
- Write an announcement for our office's newsletter to locate over-60-year-old women for a book group
- Surround herself strategically with her most positive and age-resistant friends and family members, as she prepared to launch her ventures
- And, of course, take whatever quiet time she needed to feel really ready for this next big step

So what did she do? As you can imagine, Martha's own spirit triumphed over the ageist images around her. She went on to help start something called "The Senior Class" at a local community college, wherein senior citizens paid a modest fee to attend classes. The idea was heartily endorsed by the president of the college because enrollment had decreased in response to recent budget setbacks. The Senior Class was a way to bring in a little extra revenue and keep his college in the news in positive ways. Martha's next venture after that was to become coordinator of the Gray Panthers in her local area. And, of course, her feminist discussion group turned out to be small, but feisty.

Martha's goals weren't primarily about making money, because she was lucky enough to be financially secure. But that doesn't mean that people in their sixties, seventies, and even eighties can't make a living through their own independent projects. Many will need to, in fact. It's just a matter of where you choose to put your energies. In this battle, as in all others at least to some degree, the enemies are internal. If *you can give yourself permission to succeed at being a free agent,* if you believe it can work, it will. If you wish it could but doubt that it can, you know what will happen there too.

Let Martha's projects as a senior citizen consultant, John Glenn's trip into space, and the emerging literature about the exemplary productivity of older workers be an inspiration to you, whatever your age now. There is simply no reason not to *make room* for and *give yourself permission* to have a life-enriching venture of your own, if you wish to or need to, or both. We must all trust Carl Jung's promise that "we have within us who we are supposed to be."

Open to New Possibilities

*"Man was born free,
but everywhere he's in chains."*

—Jean-Jacques Rousseau

How often do you enter a room for a meeting and head for the chair you were in last time? Or find yourself going back to the same restaurant again and again? So many of us are creatures of habit who regularly choose to do the things we've always done. That proclivity for tunnel vision is particularly problematic when you're thinking about turning things upside down (or at least a little off-center) in your working life.

Opening to new possibilities asks you to let go of those assumptions—some conscious and some unconscious—that have kept you on automatic pilot in your career. The stories below offer you some do-it-yourself strategies for getting you ready to *imagine* new things. See how college seniors Lissa and Peter, one a *gambler* and one decidedly not, react to their parents' advice about free agency. Then look at how *free spirit/rebel* Charlie manages to pry open his beliefs about himself to be able to accomplish what he wanted to. You'll also want to check out the "Openers vs. Blockers" chart in the story about Charlie to test out how likely you are to be opening up enough.

- **It's Always Something**
- **There's Something About Charlie!**
- **Forget the Mailbags**

It's Always Something!

*"Carefully observe what way your heart draws you
and then choose that way with all your strength."*

—Hasidic proverb

You'd think that the late comedy star Gilda Radner coined the phrase "It's always something!" just for budding free agents in the process of *opening up to new possibilities*. There are millions of you out there wanting to do something for yourself, but absolutely terrified to take the lid off to explore what that might be. And so, *"it's always something"* that shows up to deter you from making a space for something new. In 1998 a woman told me she couldn't think about her free agent project just yet because she knew it would be disrupted with Y2K problems and she'd decided to just wait it out. Oh well. Less dramatic variations of that dodge are still happening all over the place. Here are some of the ones I've heard lately:

- "I have some ideas, but I can't believe I'd be good at any of them."
- "How could I feel secure without my employer's health insurance program?"
- "If I started a business, all my loser relatives would want to come and work for me."
- "I would need to be sure things are going to work be fore I could get involved in some new project."
- "Who would lend me the money?"
- "It's too easy to go bankrupt on your own."
- "I'm not very good at coming up with new ideas."
- "I've heard you have to work too hard to do something on your own."

Some of these people are right—they really don't have the ingenuity, courage, and drive to be a free agent. And so for now they should plan their work lives around being employed by somebody else. But there are many of you who *do have what it takes,* and who are standing nervously in front of the free agency door, hesitating to push it open for yourselves.

There are many examples in this book and in the media of 40-something people turning to free agency as an escape from toxic workplaces or as an alternative to unemployment as they get older. We also hear a lot about college students dropping out to start dotcoms and become millionaires before they turn 30. But what's it really like for independence-loving students who are deciding whether to go the "typical" route and trudge off to work for someone else or to do their own thing? What often keeps them from following their own dreams, and what sometimes empowers them to push open that door? If you're a college student, or the parent of one, what do you need to know about the choices facing students today? Perhaps the following two stories will help.

Lissa was a senior double-majoring in art and computer science, who was preparing to interview on campus with major computer companies. A *free spirit* who happened to be quite deficient in *gambler* energy, she found herself being tossed about by indecision. Her parents were small business owners themselves, and so they actually were encouraging Lissa to use her technical and artistic skills to join the dotcom revolution.

"Go for it," her mom was saying. "You have a much greater opportunity than Dad and I ever had."

But Lissa was wary. She remembered the hard times growing up as her parents had struggled to keep their dry cleaning franchise going. It seemed like just yesterday that she had felt like the only kid in her class whose parents worked night and day to feed the family. Now she had major loans to repay and she was decidedly not wanting to worry about whether she could afford to do that. Particularly given the incredible offers that technically proficient seniors were expecting from the big companies on campus. But every time she felt she had put the "do your own thing" bug out of her mind, it popped up again—in a dream, or in a conversation with somebody.

"So why can't I just decide?" she asked plaintively. "What's wrong with me?"

"Nothing is wrong with you," I assured her, "but the collision of your high *free spirit* and low *gambler* is causing you some trouble here, making it hard for you to really *open up to new possibilities*. And there's also the problem of *either/or thinking*. Perhaps you can do both. What if you could go to work for one of these big companies right after college and then start slowly to build the idea for your own venture, saving some money as you pay down your school debts, all the while making contacts and figuring out how to make it work? Would that appease the inventor within you for a while until you feel more ready to be on your own?"

Lissa's eyes lit up. "Of course. Is that possible? Can I really interview with a company and only intend to stay for a few years? And isn't it disloyal to be cooking up my own plans on the side?"

I assured her that the average length of time in a job these days is about three years, that she could move whenever she felt she was ready—and that of course the career office would be there to help her strategize and build her own venture gradually. That's where Lissa is now, learning as much as she can with a major computer firm, but stashing money and ideas for when the time seems right to start her own venture.

Peter, on the other hand, was high in both *gambler* and *rebel,* and his professor parents were on the other end of the spectrum from Lissa's. "We want him to finish college and do graduate school," they said as they sent him to me, "but he has a wild idea about starting his own company when he hasn't even finished school. This is a knowledge-driven world, and all he knows about is computers. What will he do if it fails? Can you talk some sense into him?"

It was clear from my first conversation with this energetic 20-year-old that he had lots of sense in him already—and that he was pushing very hard on one side of the door, as his parents pushed back from the other. I asked him what his plans were for his new dotcom communications service. As I listened to him rolling them out, I was impressed. He had joined the local young entrepreneur's club and had attended the sessions on business plans, venture capitalists, and networking. He wanted to go for it, to risk losing everything, because he knew that the moment for his idea was here. If he didn't do it now, somebody else would do it tomorrow. But he also loved his parents a lot, and, as he said, "I don't want to cause them any more pain than I already have." They had endured a lot of *gambler/rebel* behaviors from Peter.

So he and I talked about the fact that sometimes doors aren't opening because the potential free agent is too frightened to push, while in other cases the pressure to stay closed is coming from someplace else (such as parents, community or religious values, or significant others). Together we brainstormed what he would say to his parents *in their terms,* so that they might better understand what he was trying to do. He prepared to talk to his mother about how hard it had been for her parents, people who didn't value education very much, when she decided to take on debt and work several jobs to get herself through a Ph.D. program—because she knew it was what she had to do.

When they finally sat down to talk it over, here's what he said: "Do you remember how hard it was for you and Gram to be angry at each other all those years? I don't want that to happen to us. And so I need your permission to do what I need to do."

As you can imagine, things were a little spicy at home for a while, but Peter's case was too compelling for his parents to hold out too long. Peter assuaged their fears somewhat by assuring them that he intended to be a lifelong learner, though probably more informally than formally, and that he was grateful to them for having instilled that desire in him. "But my path there is going to be a little different from yours," he said, "and I really need you to be okay with that."

So the historian and the English professor stepped aside reluctantly, and the door on Peter's new business idea swung open. So far, so good. He has taken a year's leave of absence from college to see what he can make happen. No matter what, Peter is pretty certain (as am I) that there'll always be a good idea just around the corner for him.

Lots of imaginative young women and men like Lissa and Peter are probably headed toward free agency, and there is no one right way to get there. There are also parents of all stripes, many of whom will push their kids in directions that don't feel comfortable to their young adult children because it's their parents' experience talking. This is nothing new. What is new, however, is the degree to which many parents' perceptions of what work is really like in the twenty-first century are too often limited and limiting. When they put their children in the position of choosing between pleasing them and functioning effectively at the unique intersection of their own temperaments and the new free agent economy, they're making a big mistake. To those young people and their parents, Andre Gide had this to say: "Do not think your truth can be found by anyone else."

There's Something About Charlie!

*"Something we were withholding made us weak,
until we found out that it was ourselves."*

—Robert Frost

Charlie was broke, but what was new about that? In the driveway and along the front of his house sat five old cars, only one of which was currently able to make it to the highway. The strange thing was that Charlie was one of the most humorous, personally generous guys you'd ever meet, and absolutely committed to being helpful to others. The only person he wasn't helping much was himself. Lots of people get to me because somebody who loves them made them come. That's how I met Charlie; his older brother made him do it.

An assistant manager in an auto supply chain, Charlie did what he had to at work to do a decent job, but that's certainly not where his energy was. But this was the "best" job he could get without a college education. His "Mr. Personality" approach to life as a young man, laced with periodic lapses of responsibility and focus over the next forty years, had brought him to his fifty-fifth birthday in a pretty depressed state. By nature a *free spirit* and *rebel*, he was allergic to schedules and deadlines. But he was also a *desperado*. Charlie fell into that "forgot to save for retirement" category, largely because he never expected to live that long. But now that he was taking his health seriously, it was looking as if he would make it to 65. And then what was he going to do?

Much as Charlie disliked his job, there was something he was passionate about—the homeless shelter his church sponsored. He was the acknowledged leader of the shelter committee, and had worked tirelessly for four years, creating a model program by establishing a county-wide coalition of Protestant and Catholic churches. Two nights a week, he also worked until past midnight getting everyone in and accounted for, and then went home to catch a few hours' sleep before going off to his job at the auto parts store. On major holidays he and his wife spent the whole day cooking and hosting events for the guests in the shelter. He listened endlessly to the stories told by the down-and-out folks to whom he ministered, assuring them of God's love and of the possibilities that lay out there for them. The men in the program loved his humor, his warmth, and his obvious belief in what he was doing.

One of the proudest moments of his life was also one of the hardest: the day when the shelter had grown large and sturdy enough to hire a "professional" director to take the place of Charlie the "volunteer." Charlie could have done the job easily—but funding and "legitimacy" concerns of the organization required that the official leader, the one on the letterhead, have the right initials after his name. Charlie was relegated to second place, still helping but not making major decisions. Charlie's unpaid sidecar had been his lifeline, and now somebody else was in charge there. It felt in some ways as if a huge door had slammed shut for him.

"So what's keeping you from getting the education you need to be able to do nonprofit administration for money as well as love?" I asked him.

"You've gotta be kidding. I feel myself losing brain power every day. If I couldn't hack school as a kid, I sure couldn't do it now. And besides, where would I get the money? My wife Dotty and I both work full-time, and there's still never enough money. Nope, it's just too late for me. It's payback time for all the opportunities and money I've wasted."

I looked at him slumping in his chair across the room,

running his hands through his thick shock of white hair, rubbing his forehead, and looking down at the floor. To be sure, he was not the picture of entrepreneurial or scholarly zeal.

I tried one of my stock energizers. "Well, I know you have two sons in their twenties. What do you think they'd like you to do next?"

Bingo. His eyes brightened. "Oh yeah, they have grand ideas all right. My older son Ted is a programmer with a major corporation, and he's after me to get my Microsoft certifications. He thinks I'd be good at it. But that's the voice of a good-kid son, not of reality, talking. My other son, Luke, is a lot like me—not much confidence in himself and a little at loose ends right now."

We went on to explore how Charlie actually felt about computers. As it turned out, he had gotten hooked nearly a decade ago when his brother had given him an old clunker. He had replaced and upgraded almost everything in it and thought it was fun. But he wondered whether old birds like him had a chance for employment in such a youth-oriented field. Especially an old bird with no college degree. "And besides," he said, "where could I come up with the money to take those courses? My credit rating looks like Swiss cheese."

Knowing that Charlie was connected more to his church than anyplace else, I asked if any of his fellow worshippers worked in information technology. Sure enough, several did. There was an opportunity for some "opening up" to occur. So, a reluctant "this is never going to amount to anything" Charlie made two calls and had appointments for information interviews within the week, to ask his friends whether they thought there was any hope for over-the-hill guys like him.

The news was cautious but encouraging. Charlie's friends from church had seen his impressive work for the shelter, and knew he could accomplish whatever really mattered to him. They assured him that if he got trained at the local community college and arranged to do some kind of apprenticeship, he'd be marketable—and they would even be willing to help him find something. As for the money, they told him he'd be able to get loans. One of his new "coaches," Warren, had another idea. "You know, Charlie, I think the place where you'd be really effective would be as an installer and trainer, helping people come up to speed with their new equipment. You'd make them laugh so much that they'd forget how intimidated they were."

Charlie practically floated home to tell Dotty about his time with Warren. They chattered all through dinner about the possibilities. But at about 3 A.M., Charlie's usual time for waking up and feeling hopeless, the old dark shadow crept in and pulled his head off the pillow again. "What kind of idiot am I?" the old voices said. "Who will lend me money, really, once they know about me? How could I stick to this training when I've eventually messed up everything I ever touched? Why did I ever let myself get my hopes up?" For Charlie, opening up was going to require letting go of his guilt and sense of failure about the past.

Fortunately, Dotty woke up too, and they talked for an hour or so. Finally, Charlie promised that he'd call me in the morning, to arrange to do some reality testing about the discrepancy between what it felt like to be with Warren in the afternoon and how he felt when the 3 A.M. terror overtook him. When we met the next week, we talked about his self-doubts and whether his church friends were being overly kind rather than realistic. I assured him that I also had seen men his age learn new skills and start over. We also talked about whether he really wanted to turn things around, both for himself and as an example for his son Luke. True to form, Charlie was willing to try for Luke's sake.

There are lots of "Charlies" in the world—terrific men and women who, for one reason or another, are finding it hard to open up to new possibilities for themselves. Sometimes this has to do with early life experiences. If you never saw risk-taking pay off for your parents or if you remember what it's like not to have enough of what the family needed, then your first impulse in tough times is probably to hold on tight. And if you've not had much encouragement about your abilities lately, it's often hard to open yourself up. For others, it's a matter of temperament (a low *gambler* quotient, for instance). Look at the chart below to see where you might fall on the spectrum of "opens easily" to "tough nut to crack."

OPENERS/BLOCKERS GRID						
(Circle the number that seems most like you.)						
Openers						**Blockers**
Optimistic	1	2	3	4	5	6	Pessimistic
Confident	1	2	3	4	5	6	Self-doubting
Energetic	1	2	3	4	5	6	Lethargic
Risk-taking	1	2	3	4	5	6	Risk-aversive
Forthright	1	2	3	4	5	6	Timid
Trusting	1	2	3	4	5	6	Fearful
Accepting	1	2	3	4	5	6	Angry
Adaptable	1	2	3	4	5	6	Rigid

All of the qualities on the left are *openers*; they make new challenges seem like fun. The ones on the right are *blockers* that keep people stuck, unable to move forward toward implementing ideas that might bring them the satisfaction they need and want. If you found yourself at a four, five, or six on any of these eight choices, you'd be well advised to start talking to somebody about it soon. There's really no reason to stay stuck here—even if you never decide to be a free agent. (See the "Openers vs. Blockers" exercise in Part Three.)

What finally happened for Charlie? After a few rounds of flagging confidence over the next four years, he found a way to blend all the things that mattered to him with his natural skills (both technical and interpersonal) to make a major transformation. After he was persuaded that if he really believed that God could make a difference in the lives of homeless men, then he probably had some plans for Charlie too, Charlie was able to ask for even more help. Along the way to his new life he worked with a career counselor, a debt advisor, a pastoral counselor, a SCORE advisor, and the academic advisor at the local community college.

And where did all that take him? With several loans and a small gift from a family member, Charlie was able to put his homeless shelter commitments on hold long enough to finish the certifications he needed to be hired three-quarters-time at a large human services agency, installing software and trouble-shooting with users. His friends at church followed through on their promises to introduce him to people. The hiring committee had loved his experience with the homeless shelter, and had enjoyed his sense of humor at the interview—"There's just something about Charlie," they told their coworkers. And indeed there was, even though it took Charlie an incredibly long time to figure that out. Eventually he was even able to get hold of the old computers whenever the agency updated, and gave them to the shelter, where he led programs for the homeless men there about how technical skills could get them moving again.

The other quarter of his paid time, meanwhile, has been spent developing his own troubleshooting/training service. One of the favorite things he does is go to people's houses, especially those over 60 who so often seemed to have missed the cyber revolution, to "connect" them to the world via computers.

Charlie's making about the same money he did as an assistant manager, when you count in the loans he's repaying. But that doesn't matter. The "collage" of his life is full with colorful designs and hopeful messages. As far as preparing for retirement, Charlie's debt counselor was able to show him how to save at least something every week, and so he and Dotty are managing the money they have differently. They're also both planning to work well beyond 65, now that Dotty is doing sidecar medical transcriptionist work at home while Charlie is at the shelter.

There really was something very special about Charlie. *And there's no doubt something special about each one of you.* If you're having trouble *opening* up to your own talents and longings and believing that they can be combined to make a new life for yourself, consider using some of the resources Charlie used to move you through step two. Talk to friends, advisors, people in your religious or community organizations, as well as professional coaches and counselors. Surf the web looking for ideas and information. Just don't give in to your fears. *Beyond this stuck place there's a life that you're not letting yourself imagine.* Let Charlie and Dotty's story convince you that Goethe was right when he observed, "The moment one definitely commits oneself, then Providence moves too."

Forget the Mailbags!

*"No problem can be solved from the same
consciousness that created it. We must
learn to see the world anew."*

—Einstein

During a time of *opening to new possibilities,* it's essential to
turn a critical eye toward your own sacred assumptions.

One compelling metaphor for people forgetting to look
around them with eyes open is provided by the story of the
first casualties on the *Titanic.* Who were they? The workers
in the ship's mailroom, who lost their lives by obsessively behaving as if the ship weren't sinking at all. As the alarms
sounded and the holds were filling with water on this
supposedly unsinkable ship, the mail crew labored single-
mindedly to drag the wet, cumbersome sacks of mail up
heavy ladders and onto the deck, to be put in lifeboats that
didn't exist. They chose not to check the realities of the crisis
at hand. One by one, they were pulled or washed back into
the murky depths below. There they perished with the mail
they were faithfully dragging to nowhere. Today, all over the
world, workers who believe that, somehow, their employers
will still maintain their Cadillac benefit plans and take care of
them as they once promised are also going down with the
mail.

So what can free agents—and potential free agents—do to
decide whether to drag the mail sacks up on deck, run for the
nearest life raft, or grab a life vest and go it alone?

Probably the best thing you can do is to start out making
a list of the *assumptions that are currently influencing the
choices you're making* (or not making). Here are some questions to help you do that. Write out your answers to these
questions in a notebook or on note cards, or you can use the

"Assumptions Analysis" exercise from Part Three of the book. You're going to need your answers in the next part of this exercise.

1. How likely is it that my job will exist in its present form in two years? In five years? What am I protecting by staying where I am?

2. Am I really enjoying my work now? If yes, what's my best guess about how long that will last? What assumptions are keeping me there?

3. How likely is it that my employer will keep the same benefit package for me until I leave here? How likely is it that I'll be rewarded at a level I feel is appropriate for my hard work and extra effort?

4. How likely is it that my employer wants to keep me enough to give me more freedom about doing my work either part-time or in a flexible mode, if I take the time to show how it would benefit the organization?

5. If I stay in my current job, who will be pleased with that decision? Who will be displeased?

6. If I strike out on my own, in either a part-time or full-time free agency venture, who will be pleased with that decision? Who will be displeased?

7. What is the likelihood that I could actually make a go of it if I dared to start a part-time or full-time venture of my own?

8. If I were independent, could I find adequate benefits?

9. How many new businesses succeed? What makes the difference between successful and unsuccessful ones?

10. What is the likelihood that I'd enjoy work more if I were doing it my own way?

11. Would it be okay not to have a nine-to-five place to go to that I call "my work"? What other options are there? Which ones might fit me?

12. What would it take to get started doing something I'd really like to do? How much money would I need?

13. What are some of the ways people have found to work on their own? See if you can list 20 titles or descriptions of new-economy kinds of work. If you need a crib sheet here, Terri Lonier offers a 20-page list of possibilities in her classic book, *Working Solo*.

So what? Now that you have the answers, what do you do with them?

First off, *share them with somebody who really cares about you and whose own agendas and fears aren't tangled up with yours!* Read aloud what you've written, and then tell the person you're with how you're feeling about what's on the page. Just sharing your answers and your reactions to what has just come tumbling out of you can give you a tremendous emotional and physiological boost. Keeping things *pressed down inside you,* on the other hand, depresses almost all your important vital systems. Studies of college students at exam time, for instance, revealed major differences in the resistance to colds and other infections between those students who were encouraged to express their feelings and those who were urged to keep them under wraps. The talkers stayed much healthier!

The next step is a big one with a small set of instructions: *Check it out.* These are among the three most important words in the world. Do your research here. Ask yourself whether what you've written about your own feelings and satisfactions seems true a day or a week later. Ask people who know you well about how they see you behaving, and about what "vibrations" they've been picking up from you. Ask people who know about insurance rates, for instance. (Yes, it's available and affordable if you work through an online purchasing group or through the free agent advocacy group Working Today—www.workingtoday.org.) Or check these things out on the Web at one of the other free-agent sites, such as monster.com's "Talent Market" (content. talentmarket.monster.com). Ask people better informed than you about your company and your field. *And ask them all if they believe your assumptions are true!*

If you're like most of the folks I've counseled and coached, the majority of your assumptions about what's possible for you are flawed in some way, built on specious data about workplace realities or on ancient behavior patterns of you and your family members. *And yet these beliefs are probably having a tremendous impact on your life and work.* They're very likely keeping you stuck in situations you've outgrown or holding you back from trying new things because of old, old fears. They have you convinced that the danger you felt as a child or young person is still real. Or that somebody's just waiting for you to make a mistake. Or that you could never be safe without employer-provided health insurance.

The bags of mail are leaning against your leg at the bottom of the steps as internal alarms sound. Should you shove them aside and get out of there, or stick around and wait for the Coast Guard because you've got it on good authority that they're coming? The choice is yours. Just be sure the information and assumptions you're drawing on are based in twenty-first-century realities rather than twentieth-century experiences and mythology.

-------------------------------------→

Imagine Your Projects

*"The real failure is not to fall short of all you
might dream, but to fall short of dreaming
all you might realize."*

—Dee Hock

Finally, after taking *time,* giving yourself *permission* to leave
old assumptions behind, and *opening* to a range of different
possibilities for yourself, you're ready to *imagine* some new
things for yourself.

You might be thinking a bit impatiently that it's time to get
down to work here, but let the stories remind you that being
playful along the way is an essential component of being
imaginative. Let Norma the *philosopher/desperado* who redis-
covered her childhood just in time, David the unfocused *free
spirit,* Molly the *imagineer* who didn't want to have to choose
between her passions, and Larry the cautious *philosopher*
show you how they all worked through this step to get a
handle on something that would really work for them.

- **Take Three Pleasures and Call Me in the Morning**
- **Kid Stuff**
- **It Just Takes Time**

Take Three Pleasures and Call Me in the Morning

"Puritanism is the haunting fear that somewhere, someone may be happy."

—H. L. Mencken

Pleasure is an essential leavening ingredient in the step three *imagining* process. But it's amazing how puritanical (translate "pleasure-deprived") many people become when they set about to create something for themselves. They make it a life-or-death situation, when just the opposite energy is needed to give it an imaginative lift.

Whenever clients come to me in either a panicked or depressed state because no ideas are popping for them, I ask them the pleasure question: What three pleasurable things are you planning to do for yourself today?

"Why?" they respond. "If I had time for pleasure, I wouldn't be coming to you in this state."

"And isn't that just the point?" I counter. "If you were enjoying yourself more, you probably wouldn't be in this depleted state."

In workshops and individual counseling sessions, I ask people to make themselves a "crib sheet" of 20 things that give them pleasure. You wouldn't believe what torture it is for most folks to formulate a list that long. After the obvious ones—"having a lobster dinner," "making love," "going shopping"—the going often gets tough. Most people *just don't think about pleasuring themselves* as one of the requirements for summoning the mental clarity, energy, and focus necessary to create some free agency in their lives—be it a multimillion-dollar business, an after-hours accounting practice, writing a children's book, or simply arranging to tele-commute one day a week. Management consultant Matt Weinstein, author of *Managing to Have Fun,* in fact, travels to many major corporations teaching work teams how to "play productively," on and off the job.

So here's what you need to do to be sure you'll have enough fuel in the tank for this *imagining* process:

- Make a list of 20 things that you can count on to bring you a sense of pleasure, lightheartedness, or relief when you need it. Make the list varied—some indoor and some outside activities, some expensive and some cheap, some to do alone and some with others, some to do at home and some to do at work or on the way there, some mind- or spirit-centered and some physical, some funny and some more gentle or centering. Go for variety, because you'll be needing quite different things at different times. Leave some space between the items, so you can make checks or put dates next to them.

- Make a copy of the list. Stow one in your desk drawer or briefcase and one in a central place at home. Make the one at home accessible to others who live there. When others know you're committed to pleasure as a life-balancing, productivity-enhancing strategy, it will encourage them to support you in that effort.

- Each day, commit to doing *at least three things on the list*. For at least the first month after you make the list, check off whatever pleasures you did that day. And if you had a great time (however brief) doing something that's not on the list, pull out the list and add it. Don't let a good thing slip out of your repertoire.

- At the end of the month, let those checks tell you where you've been getting your pleasure quotient satisfied—if you have. Hopefully, you'll have a minimum of 90 checks. Based on what you see, make some judgments about your own levels of pleasuring:

- *"Hey, I'm doing a good job."*
- *"Oops, I'm only about half there."*
- *"Oh my, I haven't a single physical thing on this list."*
- Or perhaps *"There's nothing that doesn't cost money on this list—I guess I'd better think up some free things or I'll go broke."*

Pleasure is serious stuff, especially when you're trying to create a safe space inside yourself where you can invite some wild ideas to come and play with you. Do the choices you're making in your life show that you believe and honor that fact? I usually recommend that people find themselves a "pleasure coach." I haven't met more than a handful of people who don't need gentle reminders that the best antidote to the inevitable challenges of planning a major or minor worklife change is none other than *pleasure*. Let's make one thing clear here—by *pleasure,* I don't mean addictive or excessive pleasure-mongering, because that's not really pleasure. That's a compulsion that's protecting someone, in the short run, from knowing how uncentered and unhappy she or he is. But *real pleasure* is an essential ingredient in the free agency process.

So make your list, get your pleasure coach making her or his own list, and have a great month helping each other remember to use them. If you give yourself 90 terrific pleasures over the next month, there's just no way your *imagining* process (as well as your emotional and physical health) won't benefit!

Kid Stuff

*"The supreme accomplishment is to
blur the line between work and play."*

—Ellen Langer

You'd think that *imagining* new career possibilities would be fun, a pleasant escape from years of doing work that's no longer working for you. But when I asked Norma, a pleasant-looking, almost-fifty public health researcher (who had a Ph.D., more than twenty years' experience handling complex epidemiological studies, and a subterranean sense of self-worth) to think what might be interesting for her, she couldn't do it.

Her face was nearly expressionless as she told me that fate had conspired to shut down her powers of imagination. She began the litany of what she had endured over the past ten years: a sexist supervisor who made sure she never got credit for the analytical work she did, recurrent bouts of depression which stole her energy and made her late on projects, and finally, a man-about-town second husband who had left her a message on their answering machine one morning that he had moved out to live with another woman. "You'll have to excuse me," she explained in dour tones, "but imagination is a pilot light that went out long ago for me."

Norma had a lot to be discouraged about. But reality was coming up and nibbling at her from behind, and she really did have to make some decisions about how to pick up the pieces of her life and move on. On the advice of her therapist and her doctor, she had gotten a medical leave from the government agency where she had been working to consider just where she might want to go in terms of employers and locations. At the end of three months she felt a little more rested and *theoretically* open to new possibilities, but she was clearly nowhere near ready to take any imaginative leaps.

Norma's *philosopher* style made it hard for her to rush her thought processes. Indeed, she considered and reconsidered every detail of her life. And she was clear about a few things—that she was not willing to let her work take over her life, that she wanted more meaning in her work, and that she intended to make some money. Now, there were some goals on a collision course with each other. The fact that her man had used her resources and then left her high and dry, however, introduced some element of *desperado* into the situation. It was that reality that was keeping her from collapsing in on herself. Unfortunately, but not surprisingly, since she had limped along in a major bureaucracy for nearly a quarter of a century, she was not possessed of much *gambler* energy. Boy, did she need some now!

So I went through some of the usual "what if" questions to help her summon any elements of interest that might be lurking beneath the surface of that tired facade. You may remember these imagination-boosting questions from chapter four. (And you can find them in the exercises section in Part Three too.) "Change places for a week?" I asked. Not much reaction. "What kind of books to buy?" Too tired to read just now. "Favorite charity?" Herself.

Then I got lucky. "Can you remember what you were like in about the fifth, sixth, or seventh grades? What things did you have fun doing then?"

That's when the lights went on. Norma's whole body relaxed as she looked up at the ceiling, closing her eyes ever so slightly and remembering her days as a girl in the Midwest. The youngest child of farmers outside of Ames, Iowa, she had spent her girlhood out-of-doors. While her brothers worked the machinery with their father, she and her mother had managed the flower and herb gardens. She could still remember the touch and smell of the rich dark earth, and the magic of lifting an unsuspecting earthworm into the light on the other end of a trowel. "I just loved making things grow," she said.

"So where did that love go?" I asked. She went on to explain that she had been the only girl in her junior high and high school who was really good in science. So her teachers and counselors had pushed her to go East to school and study medicine. And her biology major had eventually led her to public health. Once she had her degree, she dutifully began her career with a government agency, where she had felt imprisoned ever since. Many depressive episodes, a lackluster employment record, spiking hypertension, and two failed marriages later, Norma and her physician had decided that something about her work really needed to change.

And so on that day we sat talking about the earthworms, I could see by the look on her face that this woman needed to be playing in the dirt again. So out came the quadrant drawing. "Let's divide your life into quadrants: put your work as a public health expert with a specialty in geriatrics in two of the quadrants for now, and let's see what might go into the other two."

Of course you know one of the answers—gardening. But the other one might surprise you. Working with elderly patients through "plant therapy." Geriatric research says very clearly that older people who are exposed to gardens, plants, and trees have much better mental and physical health than those who don't. The point of plant therapy is to let older people "play in the dirt" too, to feel a spiritual and emotional connection to the earth, and somehow stay healthier in the process.

So there we were, with all four quadrants full. Norma looked like a different person—smiling, with a new light in her eyes. "But I can't do my job half-time," she said. "It's against the regulations."

"We didn't say it would be your old job—we just said you'd be doing public health work."

"Who would hire part of a person?"

"Oh my, you've really been imprisoned in the bureaucracy too long," I said. And therein began a short lesson on the new economy, on the preponderance of free agents happily making a living on all kinds of strange schedules, and on the possibilities of designing exactly the life she wanted. Norma was not convinced easily, however, and so we set her up with a schedule of people for information interviews about the unfamiliar world of part-time or contract work in geriatrics, and about the emerging specialty of plant therapy. She consulted with people who had known her for years in her field (and who were uniformly supportive of the idea of selling what she knew to a variety of interested parties rather than laboring inside a bureaucracy). She also talked to other alumnae from both her undergraduate college and her graduate school about their work, not only in public health but in gardening, landscaping, counseling, and geriatric services. Wherever she went to talk to people, she got interesting suggestions about how to develop one or more of her quadrants. And the light in her eyes kept getting brighter and brighter.

So how did it end up? Norma didn't exactly walk out the door and live happily ever after. She had some "stuff" to work through, such as why she allowed herself to be behind bars in a job that held very little joy for her for so many years, why she kept her love of the earth buried for so long, and why she had such exquisitely bad taste in men. Fortunately she had a good therapist in place to help with that part of the rediscovery process.

Thanks mostly to the networking she did through her college alumnae contacts and colleagues, Norma found that she was really quite marketable as a consultant and contract researcher in the combined areas of public health and geriatrics. She had to be willing to take a longer view on that "making more money" goal, but she was able to see that in time there was enough money to be made, particularly since as a self-employed person she could work as long as she liked. Norma sold the large, expensive house she and her fleet-footed husband had owned and moved into a much smaller one with a great yard for gardening. And she began her "plant therapy" group at the local veterans' hospital, where a good friend of hers worked. She arranged to do it pro bono for six months, in return for which she would be able to analyze the results of her efforts and, if she desired, write articles about the experience. If she got the results she expected at the end of the six months, she could then write a grant proposal to have the work funded. Fortunately, she got excellent results with her study and was funded enthusiastically to continue her work with the veterans. At last contact, her expenses were down, her consulting income was creeping up, her plant therapy was working well, and she was often blissfully up to her elbows in dirt, just as she remembered being as a kid. It's important not to assume that Norma's case was all that unusual. All over the country, people who dare to get themselves up and talking to people are finding more and more possibilities.

Limiting old perceptions like Norma's really can be diluted, and then gradually washed away, when we open up to and revisit the sacred memories of our childhoods. As Parker Palmer wisely observed, "What a long time it can take to become the person one has always been! How often in the process we mask ourselves in faces that are not our own."

It Just Takes Time

*"We need time to dream, time to remember,
and time to reach the infinite. Time to be."*

—Gladys Tabor

Creating the thing that will be your signature piece—your writing, your photography, your successful dog-walking business, your internet "b2b" (business-to-business) start-up, your sidecar consulting practice—will not come all at once. You may have learned how to get money when you need it, scrambling for odd jobs and gigs, on a just-in-time basis. But that won't work for the big things you want to birth. *Imagining* important ideas and ventures takes time.

You must also say out loud (both with your voice and on paper) what it is you're hoping to accomplish. This is terrifying, but essential. Outline it on paper. Put the paper away and come back to it in a few days. Redo it, based on what's been cooking in your head all the time that it's been lying on the shelf. When you've got it in a shape where it's not total mortification (as in "I must be out of my mind to be thinking of doing this, and this plan doesn't make any sense at all"), then it's time to share it with somebody you trust. Just be sure the person doesn't have agendas other than your own in mind. Sometimes partners, spouses, parents, and jealous colleagues have spelled early death for a number of really good ideas that were brought to them. As Brenda Ueland observed: "Families are great murderers of the creative impulse, particularly husbands." So be careful whom you choose.

But do choose! An idea or vision that hasn't been shared isn't real yet. Unless you trust it enough to tell others about it, it will stay forever where it is, in the "wishing it could be true" part of your life. And, what's more, you'll find yourself wasting the time, power, and resources necessary to make it happen because you don't really believe in it enough yourself. (You'll find a "Vision Test" exercise in Part Three to help you.)

Sometimes there are embarrassments with taking an idea out into the light of day too soon. Clients tell me frequently that the first idea they talked about didn't go anywhere, and it felt a little strange when somebody said four years later, "How's that delivery service for the elderly idea you said you were going to start?" In my own case, I still have people asking about book ideas I was testing out a decade ago but have long since abandoned. Why did I abandon them? Because talking out loud about them helped me to see what was wrong with them and that there were other writing projects, ones that suited me better, that would give me much more of what I wanted.

There are lots of ways, some unexpected, to take the time you need to find good sounding boards. For instance, *free spirit* David's small business as a toy designer came together for him after more than a year of knowing he wanted to do woodworking in some way, but not knowing quite how he would do it. His thoughts were scattered—maybe he'd do kitchen designs, maybe furniture, maybe antique reproductions. Somehow each idea seemed to slip away among the demands of his busy life, and he was left with a vague sense of discontent. Why wouldn't this thing come clear for him? What was he doing wrong?

Then his sister and nephew came to stay for an extended visit at the family homestead where he was still living. The family asked him to spend some time with the boy and so he began spending hours with his 5-year-old nephew, Todd, the two of them dreaming up interesting wooden toys. Instead of escaping from home on weekends, spending time with friends, he combined time alone thinking about and drawing new toys with periods of testing them with Todd. It turned out to be a new product focus group of the first order. David was hooked. A year later, he had his first line of toys ready for the local Winter Holiday Fair in his hometown. A year after that, he was able to quit his job as manager of the local general store—but not before he had signed them up for a hefty order for his toys, which he had been selling to them piecemeal as he made them, building up a demand for his whimsical, yet sturdy designs.

You don't have to have relatives move in and disrupt your life to find out what you could be passionate about. But some kind of alteration in the pattern of "business as usual" probably will be required for you to flesh out the thing that you want to do on your own. A weekend won't do. Nor will an hour of thinking about it now and then. It has to be regular and it has to feel serious. Your real creativity is not going to venture out into a crowded room. It will demand its own time and space.

Here are some of the other things clients of mine have been able to do after giving themselves the gift of time out from their daily busy-ness:

Rebel Molly, a 20-something TV producer, negotiated a reduced schedule with her employers that would let her work half-time for a year. During that year, she had time alone, but also got a series of photographs in shape for a major exhibit. She really didn't know when the new arrangement began whether she'd want to return to her producer's job. Molly was shocked to discover at the end of her exhibit that she wanted to keep her photography as a sidecar rather than as her full-time job. She hadn't anticipated how much she'd miss the constant intellectual and artistic stimulation of her job. For the next year, therefore, she increased her hours to four days a week, still not quite a full load, in order to have time to keep on doing photography. The TV station was satisfied because she was very good and they had her "mostly back," and she had answered for the moment the question of whether she wanted to be a full-time free agent or not.

Philosopher Larry had always been cautious about money, so even though he was living on his high school auto shop teacher's salary, he had socked away plenty. When he woke up on his 40th birthday and could hardly get out of bed, because his head felt like someone was taking a hammer to it, Larry called his friend, who was a mind/body therapist. "What could be wrong with me?" he asked. "You tell me," his friend replied. "What do you want to stop doing?" The words jumped out of his mouth. "Teaching." So there it was. With his friend's support, Larry went to his principal and asked if he could take a year's leave to get his head to stop pounding. The principal said yes and the rest is history. At the end of the year, Larry went off to his family's camp in Vermont, where he spent time alone reading, keeping a journal, listening to classical music, and generally healing from the clamor of work he hadn't enjoyed in years. In the woods of Vermont he found the courage to do full-time the thing he'd always enjoyed—working on cars—but not sandwiched in between hundreds of acting-out adolescents. His old neighbors in Vermont welcomed him back joyfully, and before the year was out, Larry was able to stop using his savings to live on because he had found enough business to support himself.

There are more than 40 million David, Molly, and Larry stories out there. But here's one thing you can count on: The ones doing the best job of creating something true to themselves are the ones who made a space and took the time to let it develop slowly. They have tested the idea to be sure they're using their own internal compass, not someone else's, and not trading one wrong fit for another. They're energetic and committed, but careful. No matter what kind of free agent motivations you might have, without a vision that's been carefully wrought in an open space, then shared with others and reworked, the success you seek will elude you.

STEP FOUR

--→

Find Resources and
Plan Logistics

*"We cannot control the parade of thoughts march-
ing through our minds. But we can choose which
ones we will give our attention to. Picture your
thoughts as people passing by the front door of your
home. Just because they're walking by doesn't
mean you have to invite them in."*

—Gladys Edmunds

Preparing for a free agency launch is just like starting any
trip——shortchange the *planning* or the *resources* and you're
in trouble! This is the time to focus on what's important and
clear away extraneous distractions. You'll see how *free spirit*
Paula had to stop letting her excessive modesty and lack of
efficacy rob her of the business success she wanted. And
you'll meet *rebel/imagineer* Doug, who had to pay attention
to his EQ (emotional intelligence) before he'd be ready to put
his applications software provider plans into action. That was
a shock for an egghead sort of guy who thought IQ was all
that mattered. Finally, you'll share the dilemma of *rebel/free
spirit/gambler* Marta struggling with whether to open her
greeting card business as a sidecar, or plunge in full-time.
Some of the strategies they used to get through this demand-

ing, often painstaking, step four may help you find your way as well.

- **Do You Really Deserve to Succeed?**
- **Have You Checked Your EQ Yet?**
- **To Leap or Not to Leap**

Do You Really Deserve
to Succeed?

*"The first problem for all of us, men and women,
is not to learn, but to unlearn."*

—Gloria Steinem

Paula came to see me about an old business, not a new one. Her SCORE advisor had told her he thought there were emotional issues she'd need to deal with before she could really make a success of her antiques and collectibles business.

I was intrigued by her story and asked why after five years she was choosing to make these changes. "It's a strange thing," she said, "but when I started thinking about buying a house last year, I was flabbergasted at how much money I was going to have to come up with, and how little I actually had. Here I was, working myself to death, spending every weekend on the road, and barely making it. So I talked about it for the first time with my women's group, and they were shocked too. Right then and there they asked me why I had spent all these years working so hard with so little to show for it financially."

"Great question," I responded. "Why had you?"

"Well, it's very complicated," she said. "In my family, it was always assumed that you did your work and the money took care of itself. From time to time I had wondered about why other businesses seemed to be doing better than mine financially when I was so busy, but I was too busy working to do anything about it. Until I decided I wanted a house."

At that point, it turned out, Paula had taken several months to think through the situation and her role in it. It had been helpful to share her thoughts with friends along the way. That's when Paula had turned to SCORE for information and advice—what would be required to make her free agency business viable as a way of life?

After a few conversations with the SCORE executive and with her friends, however, Paula agreed she really needed to speak with somebody about her own sense of "efficacy." This term refers to people's self-concepts, and how much they deep-down believe that they'll be able to create what they want for themselves. It's an important term because believing you can make things happen is the essential first step to achieving your desired result. Paula's childhood had been full to the brim with mixed messages—"Of course you can count on us to be here" and then "Oh well, Dad has decided to leave." And so she had early on put a lid on her expectations, preferring a safer "wait and see" approach. Paula, who was used to giving herself away to others and not expecting much in return, was going to need some time in "efficacy school" in order to earn what she deserved.

Her advisors were advising her to do much more of her work on the web, rather than race around the countryside on weekends and then keep her small storefront open waiting for someone to come in periodically. "But the web seems so visible," Paula told me. "I don't think I could pull it off."

"Well, let's look at your numbers for the old business— the work-yourself-to-death-for-a-few-sales approach," I suggested. "And then let's put the projections for a largely web-based business next to them. Then tell me about the difference."

The numbers spoke for themselves. "I don't know, I just don't know what's wrong with me. But I guess we do need to be talking about it."

And so Paula began seeing me for monthly coaching sessions, where we looked backward and forward at the same time. Underneath all that subservience and self-doubt was a *free spirit* with lots of good ideas, and, of course, a *desperado* frame of mind with potential mortgage lenders asking about her income. We looked back to ferret out the remaining feelings of self-doubt she had about her ability to take charge in this way. Part of charging more and being more visible felt disturbingly foreign to Paula, and so we needed to talk that through, in order for her reticence not to undermine the profitable "new" business she was trying to launch.

I asked her how she felt about money, and she said that down deep it felt tainted to her—as if she should love what she did and not want to make any money from it. We talked about her family and their views toward money. She remembered a family story about her great-grandfather, the family hero, who had been a bank manager during the Depression. The story passed on to her with pride by several generations of adoring women was that he had known the crash was coming (because he was an all-knowing male, of course) but that he had left the family money in the bank because that was the noble thing to do. And so Paula had intuited from his "sacrifice" that money was meant either to be given to others or not made at all. Of course, when we unraveled the logic of the story, it made no sense, but then family mythologies seldom do. But its impact had cost Paula a more comfortable livelihood for years. And she was determined to put that family fable to rest.

Paula has made a great start in that direction, actually. With help from a web designer and manager, she has launched a simple but effective site that she feels represents her business accurately. "No bells and whistles," she told her web consultant. "Make it seem like me." Which it does—with a newsletter, a mailing list, and enough orders to require that she hire a half-time person to fill them. Paula isn't going to get rich, because she doesn't want to. Hers is a true "lifestyle" business, where she gets to exchange helpful e-mails with her customers and to feel as if she's providing a real service. But she *can* afford a mortgage and a new truck and having most of her weekends free. That's a major achievement that would probably never have come about had Paula not decided to unlearn some childhood feelings and add on some exciting adult skills.

There are lots of Paulas starting new ventures or restarting old ones in a more strategic way. Many of them will fail or just limp along if paying attention to their underlying attitudes about *deserving to be paid fairly for good work* is not part of their basic step four planning. I constantly encounter women (and some men) giving it all away. Perhaps you've seen some of these giveaways in action:

- Charging too little for services or products
- Caring more about being "liked" than about being paid fairly
- Being embarrassed about charging what their accountants tell them they need to charge in order to make a real profit
- Downplaying their marketing and advertising so as not to be "so obvious"
- Resisting being in the spotlight for media coverage, community promotions, or online visibility
- Making self-effacing or minimalizing statements when asked about their work or their companies
- Failing to take much-needed time off to rest or upgrade their skills because their clients or customers might be inconvenienced or displeased

At its base, this is not about money or time—*it's about women (and some men) of all ages needing to take themselves more seriously.* The new free agent economy is an unprecedented opportunity to "democratize" the workplace without relying on corporate diversity or affirmative action programs, if we just have the courage to claim what is ours in our individual ventures. Cyberspace offers a level playing field in ways that corporations never can. Fortunately, Paula learned how to make this new phenomenon work for her. Buddhist teacher Alan Cohen got it right when he said, "Unworthiness is the subtlest of obstacles that stand between us and our good. It is a crafty thief that masks itself in the garb of guilt, false humility and even pride, and robs us of the full expression of our potential as Godly beings." Many of us must keep on reminding ourselves of that as we plan for success in the new economy.

Have You Checked Your EQ Yet?

*"If the driving force in the 20th century has been
IQ . . . in the dawning 21st century it will be
EQ, and related forms of practical
and creative intelligence."*

—Robert Cooper and Ayman Sawaf

Some resources that free agents will need are tangible and predictable—such as information capital, materials, workers (maybe just yourself, maybe some helpers), advisors, and plans for creating and delivering your product or service. But research shows that somewhere between 80 and 95 percent of our successes are probably determined by something we can't see at all: *our emotional intelligence.* How well you understand yourself and others, how well you communicate, how well you manage yourself in the world, will make all the difference in whether this free agency thing you're planning will work, or not work.

This can be a bit of a conundrum for free agents, who many times by nature prefer the role of loner, or resist marching to the beat of someone else's drum. For some free agents, working alone can be a way not to think about some of the competencies they're hoping they won't need in order to be successful. That's why *rebel/imagineer* Doug was in such a state when he came to see me about the idea he had developed for a b2b applications software venture. He had the idea, he had the technical skills, he knew he wanted to do it—and yet, true to form, he was having trouble getting the project organized.

So I pulled out the "Emotional Intelligence Checklist" that I often use with people considering free agency (there's a copy for you in Part Three), and asked Doug to talk about it with me.

These five composite EQ skills are actually only a fraction of the number which Goleman, Cooper, Sawaf, and others discuss in their various books and articles about succeeding in corporate America. But in my experience, they seem to be the ones that are most essential to getting a free agency venture up and running. I explained to Doug that we'd discuss the components of these items and figure out how well he felt he had mastered each of these five—so that we'd know where to start to help him check out this "soft" section of his resource checklist. I also said that he'd need to agree on a 1 to 10 "score" for himself on each of the items, with 1 meaning that he didn't feel very accomplished in that area and 10 meaning he felt he was all set there.

Here's the chart we used, and the scores Doug gave himself as we tried to understand the trouble he was having getting prepared to launch:

EMOTIONAL INTELLIGENCE CHECKLIST	
Personal Competency	**Your Score—1 to 10**
1. Realistic self-appraisal/desire to improve/confidence that you have the skills to meet your goals.	8
2. Adaptability/flexibility	9
3. Optimism/generally positive expectations about life	2
4. Self-control and follow-through	2
5. Initiative and drive	2

Well, no wonder he was having trouble—the discrepancies were amazing. He certainly knew he was smart enough, even if he had flunked out of Yale after one year. And he was adaptable enough to deal with difficult people and situations if he could ever get launched. But his life view was extremely negative, perhaps because of his experience as the only child of pretty immature and narcissistic parents, who had never given him much of anything except some good genes for IQ and too much "get lost" money over the years. His parents had both been "married" to their careers, and each had a closet substance abuse problem. There had been very little energy left for parenting, and so Doug had learned very early to spend lots of time alone, and not to expect many good things to happen. What could he really count on, and so what was the point of trying very hard? What's more, because there had not been much discipline or encouragement in his life, he had very little self-control and not much drive to get up and get moving. And so one week had led into another and then into months, and his great idea was languishing for lack of attention. He hadn't prepared a business plan as the venture capitalist at the Young Entrepreneur Conference had suggested, and he had barely scratched the surface of the demographic and economic data he was going to need.

"It sounds like you're doing to your fledgling ASP venture what was done to you as a kid," I commented.

I expected some rebuttal from him, but none was forthcoming. For a long while he just sat and stared at his scores on the "Emotional Intelligence Checklist." Finally he spoke.

"Wow, this chart does make some things pretty clear, I guess," he said. "So where do we go from here?"

"That depends on whether you really want to get on with this thing," I responded. "If you do, there are different levels of combined learning and gentle butt-kicking that we can use."

Doug convinced me that he really was ready to get moving, and so we discussed the various things he could try. Here were my suggestions: "Some people find that seminars and workshops are helpful, and I have a list of some if you're interested. Books can be useful too. I'd really recommend that you have a look at some of the EQ books on my list. For your low optimism score, I'd suggest a few sessions with a person who does brief cognitive counseling—zeroing in on the negative perceptions you're carrying around with you and how you might change those. As for the self-control and initiative items, I think we could do some coaching sessions, with goals and homework, to help you develop more of those skills."

"That sounds doable," he said. "You mean this is not a terminal affliction?"

"Not likely. Unless you're really enjoying this stuck place for one reason or another."

Well he wasn't, and so there were solutions for Doug. Just as there are for you if you're finding that the EQ part of step four is hard. Here are the things that Doug actually did to get himself moving:

- He decided to skip seminars: "You know I'm not a groupie," he explained.
- We agreed, however, that he'd postpone the specifics of planning until he felt he had a little more control over his life. Why try to fight on two fronts at once? we reasoned.
- He did read about EQ, and particularly enjoyed a book by Dan Goleman, *Working with Emotional Intelligence*. It was really useful for us to have a conceptual framework in trying to help him see how he had been giving his power away for a long time. Because Doug was such a reader (he had, after all, escaped his loneliness between the pages of books from an early age), he also decided to read Martin Seligman's *Learned Optimism*, to get a better handle on his negative "explanatory style." Reading that book, he hoped, would make therapy unnecessary—and he was in fact able to make major strides in identifying and changing his own gloomy view of the world.

- Finally, he decided to take advantage of the "gentle persuasion" of some coaching. We put him on a gradually increasing "homework" load of setting realistic goals and following through on tasks related to those goals.

In about three months, Doug was itching to get back to some serious planning. And this time he was much more ready. People don't turn around 25 years of bad habits in three months, but just naming his EQ deficits and committing to doing something about them put Doug in a very different place. "So why don't the books and courses about entrepreneurism and starting small businesses talk more about this emotional stuff?" he asked during one of our sessions.

"They do, indirectly," I responded. "But I guess words about feelings and fear and stuck places don't fit in easily with the pioneering mentality." Indeed. But if you or someone you know seems to be stuck in a step four place, unable to pull together the myriad *plans* and *resources* that will be required to get to the launch you're anticipating, you might give some thought to an analysis of where you are in your own levels of free-agency EQ competencies. Max de Pree was correct after all when he said, "At the end, it is important to remember that we cannot become what we need to be by remaining what we are."

To Leap or Not to Leap

"Nobody ever crossed a chasm in two small steps."
—David Lloyd George

"My mother's telling me to shoot the moon and just go for it, just borrow a little money and start my own greeting card business," Marta said, as she squirmed a little in the chair. I had worked with this wiry little redhead since her college days, through multiple job searches and employment crises. A definite *rebel,* she had chafed under one management system after another. Here she was just about to turn 30, tired of trying to fit into other people's organizations, and wondering how to get started working on her own, since the economic ground rules seemed to have shifted so.

She continued, "But my father doesn't agree. He thinks the best thing to do is keep my job at the bookstore, build up a portfolio of designs, and maybe even try to get the manager of the store to carry a few. It's unusual for my parents to disagree on something as big as this, so I really feel stuck. I figured you'd have some insights since you've known me so long."

Marta was not alone with this dilemma. Choosing between two options, (1) the pain of feeling imprisoned in an employee role while yearning for the autonomy of doing your own thing, vs. (2) the increased risks involved with "just doing it," is something greenhorn free agents face every day.

"It's going to be a gamble either way," I reminded her. "But if you do your research carefully, you should be able to figure out which approach will fit better with your realities now. It's not about whether to follow your mom's advice or your dad's. It's going to be about what the numbers show and what feelings come up for you during the process.

"And there's one more thing," I said. "Let's make this a clear choice. You can begin small as a sidecar venture with little debt and grow the business slowly. Or you can burst through the starting gate with enough power to really make it work within several years. But you should not consider mixing the two—starting it as your primary business *without a solid plan* or *without enough resources* is a sure recipe for failure."

Marta swallowed hard and didn't speak for a few seconds. The seriousness of the choice at hand was becoming clear to her. "Okay," she finally said. "Sounds right, I guess. Now how do I get started on this research?"

I suggested that she have two hanging file boxes, one for a major start-up and one for a sidecar venture. There would be some overlap in information to be sure, but she should investigate each option as if she were trying to decide about investing in Company A vs. Company B. I suggested she get hold of several books. (See the *Resources* section in Part Three.) She would also want to bookmark some of the best web sites for small businesses, since new ones were coming up all the time with the mushrooming of the b2b segment of the economy. Then we made a list of the people she'd need to contact for information:

- Lawyer
- Accountant
- SCORE
- Banker
- Real estate agent
- Vendors of materials—ink, paints, paper, envelopes, machines, etc.
- Insurance agent
- Web consultant

The end result of all this gathering of information, from the web to written materials to in-person conversations with a range of experts, would be drafting the rudiments of two different business plans—one for a staggered start and one for a major launch. Then Marta would be able to decide for herself which plan fit best with the rest of her life, and develop the final draft of whichever plan she chose to take to the bank.

Marta was a determined young woman, mostly *rebel,* but with a modicum of *free spirit* and *gambler* as well. I knew she'd need some help pulling her research together and resisting a premature leap. At my insistence, she arranged to use some of her extra vacation days to do her reading, explore the vast resources on the web, and meet with various professionals and vendors whose help she would need. She started off spending one whole week immersed in the information-gathering, also taking constant readings of her own emotional reactions to what she was discovering, and keeping them in a career log. I explained, "When you get to the decision-making stage, you're going to want to go back over what this all felt like to you. The decision will be made by the numbers, of course, but will also be informed by the feelings and insights that came to you along the way. So you don't want to lose them."

In about two months, Marta had her draft business plan completed. It was time to pull the process together. She knew that the SCORE executive thought she should borrow money and leap in. Her parents were holding tight to their original positions. She came to my office with her plans and her career log in hand.

"How do you feel about all this work you've done?" I asked her.

"I feel terrific—as if no matter what happens, I'll know I did a thorough job getting ready for this decision. I haven't even been anxious, really, because I believe that it's possible to begin successfully either way. I just have to decide what will fit best with my personality, and with the other parts of my life now."

And so we spent the next hour going over the data she had brought about the two different approaches to starting. Her sidecar draft plan showed that she would need to cut her hours at the bookstore to three long days a week, which her boss had said she could do. That would let her keep her health insurance and pay for her basic living expenses. She'd have to borrow only enough for materials and various professional fees, since her parents' basement was large enough to serve as her card-designing and fulfillment center. She would market her work through retailers and on the web. Her calculations showed that she could probably grow the business enough to leave the bookstore altogether in about three years.

The full launch, on the other hand, would involve renting a small space she had found on a side street downtown, not far from the local college. Her parents had agreed to cosign the first business loan, with the expectation that she'd be able to handle succeeding ones on her own. This plan would involve moving back home with her parents to save money, then spending the next several months full-time developing her inventory and creating a web site. In about four months she would be marketing and selling her cards. She would start with a specialty line geared to college students, to be marketed not only out of her little store, but also on the web. The plan would require long hours, and she'd need to get technical and marketing help (probably hiring students as well as freelancers), but it seemed that, if all went well, she could be self-sustaining in about 18 months.

Then we started looking at the paragraphs she had highlighted in her career log. As we did, some themes began to emerge. "I notice that I keep mentioning my age in one statement after another," she said, "and this feeling I have that I'm freer now than I might be in three or four years. Bob and I might decide to get married next year, and then the kid thing will press in."

"What are you feeling about the risk of borrowing enough money to do a major launch?" I asked.

"It's funny, but that doesn't bother me much. I believe that 'two small steps' thing I've heard you talk about—I have this awful image of myself taking a too small step and slipping right down into the jaws of the gorge. So it actually seems safer to take a bigger risk."

The words tumbled out of her. "So those two things come together for me now. I think it should be a total commitment, rather than designing things on the side and gradually getting them to market. And it should be now while I'm free of family responsibilities and young enough to put in those 12- to 16-hour launchpad days that all the books talk about."

We just smiled at each other. It was done. Running through my head were vivid memories of the "I want to do it my way" sophomore, the one who couldn't tolerate boring lectures and mammoth assignments, the one who was always looking for things to be different. Would this business venture give her the autonomy and the self-directedness she seemed to need? Only time would tell. But it felt like a sound decision now, informed by both data and intuition. And that's about as good as it gets in step four, *find resources and plan logistics*. Soon she'd be ready for launch!

Launch/Make It Happen

"There is no security in life, only opportunity."

—Mark Twain

No matter how you slice it, the *launch* is always a scary event. It's when the introspection and planning you've done come to fruition, but it brings the requirements that you go through one last check of everything and ask yourself the hardest questions yet about whether this thing you're about to do is really a good match for you. Honesty and self-awareness are never more important than at this moment.

The lessons in step five let you look inside the dilemma facing Erik, the *philosopher* with very little *gambler,* deciding between two equally enticing options. You'll also encounter the *imagineer/desperado* (again, with no *gambler*) Clare, who's having second thoughts about launching her own health care consulting business. Go through a "six-step reframe" with her to learn how to wrestle pre-launch anxieties to the ground. Finally, see what *philosopher* Jeffrey is going through as he comes to see that the requirements of launching his comic book partnership might not fit his own natural rhythms. But these people all handled the *launch* and you will be able to also—so long as you have a well-conceived plan that reflects both who you really are and what's needed "out there" in the world.

- **Compromise**
- **Missing Teeth**
- **Fascinating Rhythms**

Compromise

*"We have to stop figuring out what to do
by looking at what we've done."*

—Peter Senge

Erik was on his way to a conference in Boston and, at the suggestion of a friend in San Francisco, where he lived, had decided to take a detour in order to stop by my office in western Massachusetts to talk about his dilemma.

"I think I'm going crazy," he began when I asked him to tell me what he hoped to get from this session. "I feel so incredibly stuck. I'm looking at two alternatives, both of which are manageable, and I just can't decide. It's like there are two beautiful women in love with me, and I don't really want to choose. What's wrong with me—I feel like a career bigamist."

As the story rolled out of Erik, I discovered that he was a very successful director of design for a high-end advertising firm in San Francisco, and was just finishing a year's mini-sabbatical, during which he had worked ten days a month on-site for his firm. He had spent the other half of his month wonderfully alone in a small house overlooking the ocean in Sausalito. With the sun dancing through his windows nearly every day, he had created more than 75 drawings and water-colors of the Sausalito coastline, of the strange assortment of tourists against a backdrop of azure blue beauty, and of the locals gathered around listening to music in the evening. There was something in the light and colors of his pieces, in addition to his minute attention to detail, that made his work come alive. He pulled out a leather portfolio with some slides for me to hold up to the light. "These are amazing," I told him. "And you did all this in less than a year?"

"Yes, and I'm not finished yet. There are so many more inside me, pushing to get out and onto paper. And there are people wanting to buy these. But I just can't let go of my job to come and do this full-time."

Erik was lucky. His reputation in the world of design and his highly unusual "sabbatical" had positioned him to have attention paid to his work. That had paid off well, with a show in a Sausalito gallery and an article about his "arrangement" in a San Francisco paper. Inquiries about his work kept coming in. But therein lay the dilemma. Both his lovers wanted an answer—was he coming back to San Francisco to be a designer again, or was he going to move to Sausalito and be an artist? He didn't want to do either one. *He wanted to do both.* Erik's free agency profile became clear very quickly: He was high in *philosopher* (take your time, keep the peace); medium in *free spirit* (be creative, shift gears); and just about zero in *gambler* (risks, quick decisions).

We spent a little time talking about the "Options Sorter" I often use with "decidophobic" folks. (See the exercise in Part Three to try this yourself.) Erik listed the things he was looking for down the left side of a page. His list was interesting in its bifurcated nature:

- Making art
- Being with challenging, interesting people
- Being alone
- Time by the ocean
- Nightlife
- Autonomy
- Peace of mind
- Time in the city
- Being well known
- Proximity to friends and family in San Francisco

Not a bad list to work with. So next we applied the list to each of the options he was considering: going back full-time to his position with his agency or moving to Sausalito to do his own work full-time. Either option promised success. He would make more money initially if he went back to his old job, but his reputation, his talent, and the publicity that seemed to be flowing his way hinted rather loudly that in time it would not be a major financial problem for him to be an artist full-time.

"I feel so foolish," he said. "I have friends in Sausalito who would give anything to be able to support themselves with their art. Why can't I just say yes?"

"Look at your list and your scores," I said. Erik had gone down the list, ranking each option on a scale of 1 to 10 in terms of how well it matched with the desired qualities, and then adding up the 10 separate scores in each column. Something had happened that had almost never occurred when I used this grid with clients: The two options (design director or full-time artist) came in at nearly a dead heat.

"Oh my god, what now?" Erik implored.

"The numbers usually don't lie," I responded. "It seems to me you have to find a way to do them both."

"Why must you define yourself as a designer or as an artist anyway?" I continued. "When you do your designing, you make art. Not with the same intensity as when you're drawing on your deck in Sausalito, but it's art nonetheless. And look at your scores for the ocean and the city—you love them both. Perhaps the only way not to *compromise yourself* in this decision is to work out a compromise with your agency."

By that time, the session was almost over, and Erik was more than a little eager to escape. He had come for me to help him choose, and here I was telling him he probably shouldn't. So we set up some homework assignments. He agreed to do the following:

- On the flight home from Boston, make a list of less demanding roles, other than design director, that he could imagine playing in the agency—and if they didn't exist, make them up.
- For each one, create an imaginary rationale to present

to the VP for marketing to whom he reported, showing why and how the agency would benefit from his staying with the organization in a different role.

- Identify one or more persons inside the organization who could be a sounding board for his ideas.

As he left, Erik shook my hand and said, "Well, this has been a shock. I'll get back to you." I thought I saw a little spring in his step going down the stairs from my office, but only time would tell.

In fact, compromise did win the day. Both of the designers on Eric's team and the VP of Human Resources were willing to be sounding boards and advocates for his modified role. Fortunately, Erik's supervisor also turned out to be more interested in keeping Erik aboard as a designer than in forcing him to return to a 60-hour-a-week position managing the design team. For his part, Erik was willing to sacrifice money for time (as more than three-quarters of working men and women tell pollsters they are). And so they had a deal.

Erik would continue to work half-time on a flexible schedule that honored both his and the agency's needs. They agreed to trust each other that it could work out, which so far it has. He is the designer on major projects, and several other less senior people are handling the project management. This move saves money for the agency and gives them the opportunity to develop other people.

The change was not an immediate total success, as you might imagine. It took time to smooth out the client relationships and to develop a team in place of the single powerful force that Erik had been. And, in all honesty, it also took Erik some time to learn to let go of some of the hard-earned power he had to relinquish in order to have his time in Sausalito making art.

About eight months into the new arrangement, Erik called for one of his monthly check-in sessions. "How is the arrangement feeling now?" I asked. "It's fine this week," he said. "But

I have no idea how long it will last. You know what it's like in corporate America these days. It's about as volatile as it is inside the mind of a crazy artist. But que sera sera."

Absolutely! Erik really has no way of knowing how long the agency will think this arrangement works for them. And he certainly can't predict which way his own impulses will take him in another year or two, or ten. But there is one thing he does know for sure: that he has within him the vision, the courage, the confidence, and the strategic skills to think his way around the obstacles which he will inevitably encounter. He knows they're coming. He just doesn't get to know what they are. Nor do any of us.

Missing Teeth

"To venture causes anxiety.
Not to venture is to lose oneself."

—Søren Kierkegaard

Clare was visibly shaken when she came in for her "getting ready to launch" consultation early on a Monday morning. She had that "doe in the headlights" facial expression, and she could barely hold eye contact as we began the session.

"Clearly, something has happened to you," I observed. "What's going on?"

"It's about my teeth," she responded.

"Like what? Do they hurt?"

"No, nothing like that," she said, "but this is really strange. I woke up this morning dreaming about taking an overnight trip on a Russian train. Suddenly, one by one, my teeth just seemed to come loose and were spilling out onto the pillow. I jumped out of bed to look in the tiny mirror there in the train's sleeping compartment and, sure enough, my mouth had no teeth, just empty gums. My face was sunken and I didn't look anything like myself. It was unbelievable. As I woke up, it took me a few moments to be sure I was dreaming. I don't think I'm fully recovered yet." The look on her face had already told me that.

Fortunately for Clare, I was no stranger to missing teeth dreams, having led many clients through them and having had a few of my own. In fact, they show up regularly in the "literature" of dream interpretation as symbolizing fear of losing power and autonomy. To be toothless in the primitive world that spawns dreams was a pretty serious thing, so there was evidently something frightening going on for Clare. We talked about how dreams bring to the surface the things we need to be considering. Clare's unconscious mind had known she would be on her way to speak to me that morning about how things were going with the sidecar health care consulting practice she was about to launch. What better time for her unconscious mind to call to her attention the feelings that were undermining her forward progress?

"You know, Clare," I told her, "the last few people who have told me about their toothless dreams have been wrestling with questions about their own power and wondering about their ability to control the problems that their new ventures would undoubtedly bring to them. I wonder if that's what *your* tooth dream was trying to get us to talk about?"

She nodded. "I think so."

And so we started making our way through the questions that I usually ask about the vivid dreams people bring to me. (You can also find a copy of these questions in Part Three for your own use later.)

Perhaps you have a recurrent or recent dream (missing teeth dreams are obviously not the only juicy ones in need of understanding) that you'd like to run through this analysis. You can consider the questions yourself, or with a friend or family member. Or, if you're lucky enough to have a trained counselor of one kind or another at hand, you can discuss the dream with that person. The one thing not to do is just forget it—because you can bet it will return to try to get your attention some other way. So have a try at these questions:

1. Now that this dream has shown you that your unconscious is wanting you to think about or get some help with a situation, do you have any idea what it wants you to talk about today? Sometimes it will be obvious, other times not.
2. What feelings do you remember having during the dream? What was the dominant feeling at the end of the dream? What particular images or words grabbed your attention?

3. What internal fear, doubt, or uncertainty did the vividness of the dream bring up for you?
4. What external, practical questions or considerations are
   you wrestling with now in your work decisions that
   might be related to the feelings of the dream?
5. What good news is there for you in the dream?
6. Let's look at each *fear* and each *practicality* you men-
   tioned, one by one, to determine what's a valid warning,
   and what's probably *about your own self-protectiveness
   being stuck in overdrive.*

As Clare and I discussed her dream, it turned out that she
had been thrown off-balance the week before by information
about possible new restrictions on consulting contracts at the
hospital where she was employed as a nursing supervisor.
Even though she had a public health degree in addition to
her RN, and tons of ideas (she was an off-the-charts *imagineer*), she was scared (nary a trace of *gambler*). So she had
begun over the weekend to question the plausibility of her
whole plan to transition gradually from being a nurse manager to being a health care consultant. She feared that these
changes in rules at that hospital did not bode well for some
of the contracts she was hoping to get at other hospitals and
HMOs.

Her *desperado* situation, being a recently divorced mother
with very little child support available, wasn't making this any
easier. So there was in fact something to worry and do some
strategic planning about—but certainly not enough to lose
her teeth over. The good news from the dream was that, just
as she was struggling awake, before she got over to the mirror, she had seen tucked into the compartment drawer an
old-fashioned card that read "Dentist Available." There was a
subtle clue that help was out there if she would just seek it
out.

And so we took the time to look at both the internal and external dimensions of Clare's concerns. She had been known to

wrestle with anxiety from time to time, so why should we think that her gradual transition from being on payroll in a secure (or *supposedly secure*) role to eventually taking full responsibility for generating her own income would come without a hefty dose of fear? In order to help quiet her feelings of being out of control and vulnerable in this new venture, Clare agreed to do a Neurolinguistic Programming visualization called a "Six-step Reframe" with me. In this exercise we arranged for her creative problem-solving self to have a conversation with an unconscious part of her that was holding her hostage to her fears.

In the visualization, her unconscious was reflecting the concerns of her mother, who had somehow believed that the one best way to make one's children feel loved was to worry about them constantly. Following my directions, Clare dreamed up several positive alternatives to this incessant and debilitating worry. She considered finding a health care consulting firm to join as an employee, as well as waiting several years to get some more money put away. But she selected the one she felt best about—going ahead to start her part-time consulting practice, and enlisting the help of a well-connected friend in administration at another hospital to help her stay informed of impending legislation and policy changes. Clare asked her unconscious "mother" energy to trust that she would be able to stay on track for her launch and succeed if she surrounded herself with good advisors. And the "mother" in her unconscious agreed. Clare also decided that she could reassure her internalized mother-worrier by periodically picking up an imaginary phone and telling her how well things were going.

Once Clare's fears had been quieted, it was time to examine the external dimensions of the situation—and whether or not the impending changes in policy in one hospital needed in fact to be an insurmountable problem for her consulting practice in general. As it turned out, the new regulations were never passed. But the fright did get Clare to do more extensive planning about the different kinds of problem-solving she'd be able to offer her organizational clients. At the suggestion of her colleague to whom she had turned for strategic help, she also decided to contract with a health care marketing specialist to keep her informed of potential roadblocks and to help develop more long-distance markets for her services.

Clare's situation is not unique, or even unusual. For many free-agents-in-the-making over the years, vivid dreams, the toothless ones and otherwise, have been a wake-up call to look at their feelings, thank their unconscious minds for alerting them to a possible danger, and then make the practical adjustments necessary to keep their ventures growing. Clare hated the thought of extensive marketing, so she was glad to be getting help with it. Others have needed help with different aspects of their new roles—accounting, advertising, organization, ghostwriting, research, time management, even an "image consultation." Dreams (and nightmares even) have often been the catalyst for forcing neophyte free agents to take a closer *pre-launch* look at themselves and make the adjustments necessary to succeed.

Here's some reassurance for you: For most of you, your unconscious minds are really on your side. They can be a little overreactive at times, to be sure, but they have a good nose for potential problems. You are well advised to welcome their admonitions (whether they come to you as hunches or frightening dreams), and then do the internal and external research that may be required. What you *must not do* is just *give in* to the fear and self-doubt on the way to your dreamed-of destination, whatever that might be. Scary dreams are meant to *move you forward in a more informed way,* not stop you in your tracks.

Fascinating Rhythms

"It's never too late—in fiction or in life—to revise."

—Nancy Thayer

One of the most important things about getting ready for a *step five launch* is being sure that the thing you're about to do matches your own natural rhythm. It seems so unimportant, this thing called rhythm—we'll just do what has to be done, many people say, whether it fits or not, and things will work out okay. Would that that were so.

For a little background, let's look at a story about rats, the experimental psychologists' best friends. Robert Ader, the father of psychoneuroimmunology (fancy name for the body/mind connection), was doing an experiment showing the cause/effect relationship between rats' tendencies to secrete a chemical called pepsinogen, and their likelihood of getting ulcers. Everything was going perfectly for Ader: The high pepsinogen rats who were being stressed with physical tasks were getting ulcers right on schedule, and the low pepsinogen ones weren't. His theory was right, he concluded!

But then one day he noticed that some of the low pepsinogen rats had developed ulcers. How could this be? Finally, Ader figured it out, when he assessed the natural activity cycles of those rats. Rats, it seems, like people, have preferred high and low activity cycles. The low-pepsinogen but ulcer-ridden rats had gotten into the trials in the wrong energy cycle—so that they were being *doubly stressed* by doing the highly demanding exercises in a time during which they preferred low activity. They were "morning rats" being forced to do "late night rat" tasks. And their bodies let them know they didn't appreciate it by giving them an ulcer.

So it is with people. *How about you?* Will the launch of your free agency venture bring with it expectations about activity and speed you'd rather not meet? Ask yourself these questions: When do you prefer to be active? And how active do you want to be? What's your most comfortable speed? And do you want to be "paced" by colleagues, or to go at your own merry (or less-than-merry) speed? Do you want to be alone most of the time, or with others, or perhaps have a balance of group and individual activity? (To do this in more detail, see the "Right Rhythm Check" exercise in Part Three.)

Not only do your interests, skills, and values have to match the work requirements of what you're trying to launch—but your preferred pace and rhythm must too! This is particularly true for free agents, in either full-time or sidecar ventures. You can't afford to be taking on roles that require you to run at a speed that doesn't work for your mind and body, no matter how much you might like to be involved in that kind of venture.

That's the situation in which *philosopher* Jeffrey found himself, as he got ready to launch a small comic book business with his cousin. From elementary school on, Jeffrey had loved comics, and could cite writer, publisher, dates, characters, and major themes from every major strip (plus more than a few marginal ones). He had always dreamed of getting paid to be around comic books. So when his cousin Larry proposed that he leave his job as an accountant so that he could help run the business side of a comic book venture, Jeffrey thought he had died and gone to heaven. Larry had chosen well in many ways, because Jeffrey was able to do the financials, write a business plan, and generally figure out how to make the business run. Larry was to be the marketer, the public relations guy. That sounded good to Jeffrey, for whom the rather sedentary life of an accountant had been a little boring sometimes, but rhythmically a good match.

But, a month before the store was slated to open, Jeffrey showed up in my office almost trembling. "I've made a terrible mistake. I don't think I can go through with this. There's no way we can get this business launched without both of us being out there hustling. I can see that now. But I've had a pounding headache for days and I've been up every night this week just thinking about the cold calls Larry's planning for me to do. This is not what I bargained for."

Indeed, almost everything worked for Jeffrey—the values, the interest, and most of the skills. But the life rhythm that Jeffrey needed to feel in balance each day (a slower pace, time to really talk with people, time to rest between projects) did not include running around making contacts, arranging interviews, returning frantic phone calls, and delivering fly-ers. He was at a critical juncture. Should he bail out altogether and make his oblivious, multitasking cousin furious with him, or try to forget the symptoms he was having and inhale ibuprofen to keep on going? Or was there something in be-tween? "And what's wrong with me anyhow?" he added plaintively.

"It's the rhythm thing," I said as I looked across my desk at his miserable face. "You've just got to make some compro-mises about the pace of what will be expected of you." And then I explained about the morning rats and the night-owl rats. It was actually rather easy to fix, once Jeffrey gathered enough courage to explain what was going on to high-flying Larry. They were able to get one of Larry's friends and an in-tern from the undergraduate business program at the univer-sity to come on board as contract workers and help with the launch. Jeffrey, who was more careful with money than Larry, agreed that he would absorb some of the extra cost of this help, in return for not having to play the more external role during this start-up time. He would also do more of the research and tracking components of the enterprise. His headaches went away, and, amazingly, he slept peacefully through the night before they opened the doors of their small shop and went live with their web site. Finally, the rhythm was as right as the dream of working with comics.

The rhythm question can go both ways, of course. It's not always about slowing down. Over the years, I've helped many folks understand how adjusting their speed up or down and tinkering with their work environment before *launch* can make all the difference in designing their own work. All of these free agency trainees had to make adjustments before they could actually launch their ventures:

- *Free spirit* Lindsay was an athlete and musician with an itch to start her own online company. She loved being in constant motion. When it came time to write her business plan and take care of all the details for launch, however, she found that she needed a partner who could sit still long enough to make it happen.
- *Imagineer* Parker had a thousand things going—he was always in a hurry and definitely not a detail man. In order to launch his international ski vacation business successfully, he decided to contract out the nitty-gritty planning parts to a trusted family friend. Since the bank was requiring Parker to put up a big chunk of his father's money to get the financing he needed, getting somebody in on the deal with a more focused style and slower rhythm made everybody a little less nervous.
- *Gambler* Margot got her free agency venture started, in fact, because of a rhythm problem. She was about 18 months into a coveted Wall Street stint, one that had been a "logical" choice for a magna cum laude economics major and class president, when she came down with mono for the third time. Clearly, something wasn't right. She wasn't afraid of working hard, or of taking chances— but her body was making it clear that she just couldn't do those 90-hour weeks. The answer for Margot was to return to her university town and open her own financial planning practice, where she created a particular niche with younger investors.

So when you're in step five launch mode, take a few minutes *before you leap* to check whether the pace and style to which you're committing are really right for you. Golda Meir once shared this warning to herself: "I must govern the clock, not be governed by it." That's certainly true for free agents— while you're designing this new life for yourself, remember to factor in the rhythm question. Or your body could make you pretty miserable.

---→

Fine-tune and Make Changes

"Failure is the opportunity to begin again more intelligently."

—Henry Ford

It's launched, finally. I'm doing things my way. Surely, this is going to last forever. Not so fast! Count on things needing to be fixed and changed, i.e., *fine-tuned,* every step of the way. The lessons in step six demonstrate how to make in-flight changes to keep yourself on course.

You'll meet Hal, the *rebel/free spirit* vendor of pet services, and Charlotte, the *gambler/imagineer* dynamo who nearly ran her sidecar off the road from trying to do it all. You'll also have a chance to think about turning your mini-tragedies into successes, as I learned to do during a particularly challenging period in my life.

- **It's Just Too Much**

- **Running on Empty**

- **Finding the Opportunity in the Problem**

It's Just Too Much

*"Solo work is a series of experiments.
It is not a single path."*

—Harriet Rubin

It's called a "good problem"—the day you wake up and realize your free agency venture has taken over your life as much or more than your super-demanding old job ever did. It's "good" because it means you're attracting customers or clients and, hopefully, the money as well. It's a "problem" because the state of overwhelm and running on empty you're feeling will surely limit your effectiveness as a free agent, and even do you in sooner or later. This is increasingly true for dotcom start-ups, where stressed-out young entrepreneurs are wondering how long they can keep up the pace. This sixth step of the free agency process is critical because it happens to nearly every free agent—*rarely can you get it just right when you launch.* There's always some *fine-tuning* involved.

It came as a shock to Hal when, just a year into Hal's Happy Pets, he began to feel worse than he had as a veterinary assistant at a busy clinic. He was making money, to be sure, but he was exhausted, cranky, and not having much fun at what he thought would be a joyful venture, offering pet grooming and training services in his town. Hal felt out of control, a condition which doctors and psychologists alike have pinpointed as one of the primary causes of work-related stress and illness. "It's just too much," he groaned. "Have I made a terrible mistake?"

"It's too soon to know that," I responded. "Let's talk about what feels wrong to you, and then we'll have a better idea." And so the formerly bright-eyed and outgoing young man— who had left his demanding job as a veterinary assistant because he disliked taking orders, didn't agree with the policies he saw in practice, and needed to make more money without giving up being around animals—began his litany of complaints.

"I'm just too tired. I respond to calls all the time and there's just no time for a life. My fiancée, Sue, is furious at me. Even my own dogs are mad at me when I leave them so often and come home smelling like other people's pets. I just can't seem to say no, because I'm so scared that if I turn down a request for some early-morning or weekend or later-evening service they'll never call again. Once I get there and do the work, I enjoy doing it, but on the way home I'm a mess when I realize it's late, I haven't done my book work, and I just want to fall into bed. You wouldn't believe my desk—there are half-written invoices and stray checks all over it. I feel as if my work is running me. Now Sue, who thought this was a dumb idea to begin with, is demanding that I get a 'real job' again before we think about getting married. Do you think she's right?"

"It's not what Sue thinks that matters most here," I reminded him gently. "Let's see if we can find out what you are really thinking and feeling. Are you tired of the work? Would you prefer to be working with animals in a hospital setting again?"

"Oh no—I love the freedom of making my own decisions about grooming and training animals, and I much prefer healthy animals to sick ones. It's a real thrill when I get to help someone figure out why a pet is acting strangely."

"Then what's the problem?"

"Like I already said, *it's just too much.*"

"That's relatively easy to fix," I said, "if you're willing to exercise some discipline, set some boundaries, and stop worrying that there aren't enough customers and clients out there for you. Are you willing to give that a try before you decide to chuck the whole thing?"

Hal agreed, and over the course of two more sessions we

worked out a "take back your life" formula for this combination *rebel, free spirit,* and *desperado.* He needed ways to capitalize on his resourcefulness and creativity, yet impose some
order and focus. We discussed a wide range of options. When
the plan seemed ready for unveiling, we decided that he
should bring Sue along to the session to try to get her buy-in.
Here's what Hal agreed to do:

- Get a separate phone line for the business, so that he
  could take messages there and keep his personal line,
  which would be unlisted, free from business requests.
- Limit his hours—make it clear in his advertising and in
  responses to requests that some times were off-limits
  (he chose Tuesdays, Saturday afternoons, and Sundays
  as days when he had no appointments and returned no
  calls). Since Hal worked out of his own van rather than
  in an office setting, he was in a position to exercise even
  more control than he had been courageous enough
  to do.
- Increase his prices by 10 percent this year, and then another 10 percent next year. This was likely to trim some
  customers from his list (no pun intended), but would
  increase his hourly return on investment. He had priced
  himself low to grab a share of the market, but that strategy was working too well.
- Hire an office organizer to come into his home work
  space and help him set up systems to stay on top of the
  management details. Once things were more under
  control, it was likely that the state of overwhelm he was
  experiencing would decrease. Recent stress research
  shows, in fact, that a cluttered work space sends stress
  levels skyrocketing even more than they already are.
- Hire a local high school student or stay-at-home mom
  on a casual or as-needed basis to do his record-keeping,
  mailing out of bills, follow-up calls, ordering of sup-
  plies, and booking appointments for him. That would

cost him a few dollars, but make a huge difference in how burdened he felt by the "administrivia" of keeping his practice going. We discussed some of the online business services available, but he decided that the more personal touch suited him better.

- Pay attention to his S-E-L-F care (sleep/exercise/love/food) in a vigorous and committed way. Invite Sue to help him put together a schedule for exercise, play, and togetherness, as well as a reasonable regimen for sleeping enough and eating well.

"So do you think that will do it?" Hal asked eagerly.

"I'm not sure—you won't know till you test it out. I only know that these strategies have worked well for hundreds of other free agents working their way through *fine-tuning* the inevitable static of step six."

A little on edge, but eager to try anything to feel better, Hal went home to put the new plans into action. Sue wasn't completely convinced that Hal shouldn't be looking for another job with health insurance and a regular paycheck, but she was glad to be included in the solution. She particularly liked the "love" part of his S-E-L-F help plan.

So what happened? It actually did turn out to be possible for Hal to keep his successful business going and yet carve out some time for having a life. Hal's next-door neighbor, a friendly, well-organized former officer manager who was choosing to stay home with her two small kids, was willing to help him out with both the organizing and the practice management. (Asking her had been Sue's idea.) And "casual" and "as needed" fit her life just fine, particularly since she was so close by. She was also able to help Hal get the word out about the fee increases that made him uneasy, preparing new flyers with the higher rates and responding to messages from clients as they came in. Because of the additional costs for help, Hal's net income decreased a little, even with the rate hikes, but it was more than worth it to have a life.

The S-E-L-F part? That was harder, as Hal had become rather accustomed to using himself up. I suppose you can get away with that a little longer as an employee, but as a free agent, you just can't afford to dribble away your energy and creativity on sloppy habits. Fortunately, he had Sue to help with the implementation, so even that part of the contract got attention.

"I'm so glad I stuck it out and was able to get things all fixed," Hal told me when we met for a "checkup" about six months after the new plan had gone into effect.

I laughed. "So you think this is a final fix? This is a lifetime process of tinkering with the mix of things in your life, my friend. Keep those tools handy. You're sure to need them again."

Running on Empty

*"The healthy and strong individual is the one who
asks for help when he needs it. Whether he's got an
abscess on his knee or in his soul."*

—Rona Barrett

Charlotte was a go-getter, to say the least. In my office she sat on the edge of her chair, her body seemingly on full alert, twitching slightly, as she told me of her fledgling web design and management business. She was "wired" to do it all, and had come to me because her husband Lenny, whom I had seen previously and who was now finishing his MBA at night, was worried about the hours she was spending, both on her full-time job as communications director for a state agency and as the "mother" of a new sidecar web design and management business. An *imagineer,* she had what seemed like an endless supply of great ideas for her clients. As a somewhat impetuous *gambler,* moreover, she didn't shrink from risks. So here she was, with two full-time lives running at full throttle.

"So tell me about what's keeping you going at such a frenetic pace," I asked.

"Well, there's just so much to do. I don't really feel we can afford for me to leave my job with the state until Charlotte'sWebs.com is making enough money to support my half of the household expenses. So I work about 45 hours a week at my "real" job, and another 30 to 40 building the business. I just keep on pushing, and somehow it all gets done. I feel tired a lot, but my nervous energy gets me through it."

She was speedy all right—practically jiggling there before me. Then I asked the obvious, "Does Lenny agree that you need to be putting the same amount of money into the communal coffers right now?"

"I never really asked," she confessed. "I just figured that was the original arrangement and we'd stick with it."

"And tell me about Charlotte's Webs," I continued. "How is the venture going?"

I saw a brief flash of pain in her eyes, as she told me, "Well, that's a bit of a problem. *But nothing that can't be fixed with a little more effort, of course.* I just need to give it more time. I just lost a major client this week because I was on a big project for my office and had to do a B+ rather than an A job designing and installing a secure site for one of my new clients."

As we talked, I was reminded of Charles Handy's observations about the two types of business errors: (1) getting it wrong and (2) not getting it quite right enough, missing opportunities to do the best possible job. Charlotte was into #2, robbing herself of the ability to do a terrific job in her sidecar business because, for a variety of reasons, she didn't feel able to let go of her full-time job.

I decided to ask her about that. "You're a gutsy woman," I said, "a real gambler—you just started up this venture because it seemed like the right thing to do, and now you're feathering your own engines. How come?"

As she spoke, the underbelly of her *gambler* energy emerged. "Well, I'm not sure I thought it through carefully enough," she said. "I probably should have had some more capital behind me before I took the leap. I never anticipated how worried I would get about 'not having enough.' And Lenny and I should have talked a lot more about the impact of the business on our lifestyle. But now I feel locked into having to do it all."

"And it's not working so well, is it?"

"I guess not," she answered, as tears filled her bright eyes.

A few moments later, she was crying quietly. That was a breakthrough moment for Charlotte, who seldom allowed herself to slow down or get off-course, much less to cry in front of somebody. Moving into that space of softness and vulnerability opened up by her tears, I suggested that she have a conversation with Lenny that night about her "scarcity" anxieties, and her fear that she had jumped too soon into the business. And I asked her to do something that was very hard for her: to let Lenny take care of her emotionally for at least this one evening, as a prelude to letting him help choreograph the shared dance they'd need to do to get through this.

She was surprised, and a little put off by the implication that she might not be "doing it quite right" as a partner. But she agreed to stay with her vulnerability, and to invite Lenny into the closed and demanding environment she had constructed for herself. As expected, her conversation with Lenny that evening was teary and long. But when it was over they had agreed to some startling changes:

- That they were in this together and would both work on the Charlotte's Webs business, with Charlotte doing the computer work and Lenny taking on the business details of marketing, customer service, accounting, banking, and the like.

- That they would arrange for an equity line of credit on their house, in order to buy them some time to build Charlotte'sWebs.com. In the meantime, Charlotte would give three months' notice at her job and Lenny would stay on for at least a year or so in his job as a branch manager for one of the local banks. They would have three months of both salaries to get a little more socked away and to accept some of the credit card offers landing in their mailbox each day—just for a rainy day cushion. (More than 80 percent of entrepreneurs report in polls that they used home equity and credit card debt to get their businesses up to speed.)

- That Charlotte, the *gambler,* with some help from her banker husband, would put more time into objective planning and less time into worrying about "running out" of money and time. "There is plenty to make this business successful" they agreed to remind each other on a daily basis.

- That Charlotte, the *imagineer,* would keep a log of the business tasks she did and how long they actually took, so as to get better at predicting time (and hence making her pricing more accurate).

When I next saw Charlotte, she was just about to leave her old job. She and Lenny had worked hard on a business plan and had just gotten an endorsement from the local Chamber of Commerce. "I never dreamed that working together on this would bring us closer together," she confided. "I guess I was always afraid that we'd disagree and fight if we tried to work together." Her employer had tried hard to get her to stay, but when it was clear that she would be leaving, the agency director decided to post her old job at a lower level and keep some funds for outsourcing much of the agency's web management work to Charlotte's Webs.

"It really is amazing," Charlotte said finally, "how things can open up in unexpected ways when you convince yourself to check out what's not working and ask for a little help."

Finding the Opportunity
in the Problem

"Life sends us many opportunities,
brilliantly disguised as problems."

—Marilyn Ferguson

I remember vividly the first time (the first of many) that Marilyn Ferguson, author of the groundbreaking book *The Aquarian Conspiracy,* changed my life. It was early into my sidecar years—when I was working full-time as a public school guidance director, struggling a bit to manage counseling and consulting clients on the side, and trying to finalize a research protocol for my doctoral dissertation. I had submitted a megaproposal to the National Science Foundation for a quantitative study of the development of expressive and instrumental qualities in young women and men, one that would involve hundreds of subjects, through both surveys and interviews, and a huge amount of data analysis. I had enlisted the support of my dissertation advisor as the co-investigator, and we were ready to go. As notification days drew near, anticipation ran high.

I arrived home from work one day to find that a fat envelope had arrived from the NSF. In the world of college admissions, a fat envelope is a good sign, so I was delighted. I ripped it open eagerly, expecting to find a note of congratulations and instructions for how to move ahead on this project. (That was my overactive *imagineer* speaking.) I read the first line.

"We regret to inform you . . ." and thereupon followed a devastating letter tearing apart every aspect of our grant proposal. To be sure we got the point, the letter was underscored by in-depth comments from no fewer than nine readers, each of whom managed to hack apart savagely whatever self-esteem I had left. I could barely catch my breath, and retreated immediately to my bed, where I lay mostly in a fetal position for the next 24 hours.

I tossed and turned fitfully, convinced that the world had come to an end. What would I tell my co-investigator, my doctoral advisor? Would she regret that she had agreed to cosign this dreaded document with me and no doubt tarnish her reputation as a researcher forever? People knew I had applied for this grant—how could I face them with my failure? Would I be unable to finish the doctoral program? Was my life plan forever altered? (There was a lot of "forevering" that night.)

The next afternoon, the friends who had previously convinced me to attend Marilyn Ferguson's lecture called to inquire about when to pick me up. I explained that I was in no shape to go anywhere because of this terrible, life-upending news and perhaps they should go without me.

"Are you kidding?" they responded. "This is what you need to hear more than anything. Get out of bed, we're coming over."

And so, two hours later, in a large college lecture hall, buoyed up on both sides by people I knew really cared for me, no matter how much a loser the National Science Foundation thought I was, I listened intently to Marilyn Ferguson. A few minutes into her talk, I was sure she was looking directly at me as she asked, "Just what new opportunities have you been handed recently? What unexpected openings for change are your disappointments and failures now allowing you to consider?"

Heads to the right and left immediately swiveled to look at me. *So there it was.* No wonder they had been so insistent on bringing me to hear this. I couldn't answer the question completely right that minute. But within several days I could.

Once I allowed myself to move beyond the feelings of

shame and failure, I knew that the NSF grant proposal had grown way beyond where I had wanted it to go, really, and would have committed me to a multiple-year in-depth scientific project for which I was poorly prepared. The opportunity at hand was to design a much smaller, simpler project that I could finish quickly and get on to the things I needed to do next—a project that would balance my activities in a less grueling way. Little did I know then that within the year I would be on my way to a new and very different job at Smith College, dissertation almost completed. Had the *"lettre terrible"* from the NSF never arrived, I would have remained tied to that project for who knows how long. And I would never have opened my eyes to the other things I needed to be doing.

I often remember those days, when I traveled so deep into the jungles of my own fear of inadequacy and emerged on the other side, thanks to a piercing question from that wise woman, Marilyn Ferguson. And I have gone there many times since. I have a mental picture of her with me whenever I speak with people whose career lives seem to have hit a snag, and I ask them some version of that question, "So what does this problem, this felt disaster, now give you an opportunity to do?" *This is the quintessential step six query,* to which people always have an answer, eventually.

Here are a few of the fine-tunings, reevaluations, and changes other people have managed, because they looked for the opportunities in their problems:

- "At first I was panicked when I started to dislike the business my friend and I had started. But there was the problem—how I was trying to handle growth. Now I handle just the communications and am able to do a lot of it from home, and we've brought in a hard-charging organizer type to do the operations. This new strategy works better for all of us."

- "Not getting into law school was a blow to my ego at first, but it actually gets me off the hook—now I can keep my paralegal job and do more of my own writing on the side."
- "My partner left the business when things got tough. At first I was lost—but now I realize I can take it in the direction I wanted to go anyway."
- "I've loved being a therapist in private practice. But managed care just doesn't work for me, financially or philosophically. So I've cut back my practice and am working part-time as an inside consultant for a company that has just acquired another one with a very different culture. Talk about blended family problems! I would never have explored this kind of option had managed care not been such a pain."
- "I've really liked having my own accounting practice, but now I'm ready to work for somebody else for a while, and not have to worry about marketing and organizing the business. In another ten years I'll probably want to be on my own again, especially as I head into my sixties, but for now some time under somebody else's umbrella seems just right."
- "I can't believe the business expansion we worked so hard on didn't fly. But, you know, now that I think more about it, I'm not so sure I really wanted to get that much bigger anyway. Staying smaller and more specialized feels much better."

Do any of these ring true for you? Is there an opportunity to change something in your life that's trying to get your attention? Having things become derailed or uncomfortable is as much a part of being a self-directed free agent as getting something going in the first place. But it's hard to convince people of that in the middle of the process. Hopefully that won't be true for you—you'll know when the hard times come that *there's an opportunity in there somewhere,* a chance to reevaluate what you've been doing and make essential changes. Airplanes are off course 90 percent of the time, and are brought back to the correct trajectory again and again by course-correcting software. *So too with our journeys.* Our discomfort alerts us when we've drifted from our internal desires, or failed to read the external signals well enough. Our mistakes and miscalculations are in reality our dear friends, which we must appreciate and embrace. "Let your life speak," an old Quaker proverb instructs us. Let your life's hard moments, your times of confusion and despair, speak to you of what you need to be doing and where you need to be going next, in order to follow your own path.

STEP SEVEN

Reevaluate and Consider More Change

*"If you have made mistakes . . . there is always
another chance for you. . . . You may have a fresh
start any moment you choose, for this thing
we call failure is not the falling down,
but the staying down."*

—Mary Pickford

Sometimes the changes in step seven are huge, and sometimes they're hardly discernible from the *fine-tunings* of step
six. What matters is the taking stock, considering both internal and external factors, to be sure that the thing you've been
doing is really what you should be doing now.

In this section, you'll meet Paul the *philosopher/imagineer*
engineer turned entrepreneur wrestling with what to do
about his soon-to-be-bought business. You'll hear as well
about Peg the *free spirit/gambler* and her business partner
Ninya, whose life stage issues now have her wanting very
different things than she did before. Ninya's *philosopher*
style will play itself out very differently from Paul's. We'll
also take a look at writing, and why so many people end up
doing it as part of their step seven experience, as well as why

free agency is enhanced by a "daily practice" of one kind or another.

- **The Clearness Committee**
- **It Seemed Like a Good Idea at the Time**
- **And What About Writing?**
- **Daily Practice**

The Clearness Committee

*"Until you make peace with who you are, you'll
never be content with what you have."*

—Denise Mortman

Paul sat with his head in his hands as he told me how sick
he had been for the past month. I asked him what was making him sick. "I think it's about money," he said.

"Ah, I hear a lot about not having enough money."

"No, no, it's not too little. I think there's too much."

With that, Paul began his *reevaluation* story. "You see, I've
always puttered around in a workshop. As a kid my grandmother called me 'Puttering Paulie.' So I became a mechanical engineer and on the side just invented little things. About
five years ago, I figured out a way to filter the impurities from
computer 'clean rooms' and started manufacturing machines
for local businesses. In less than a year I was able to quit my
job, and now the thing has grown so fast that I have three options facing me. I can keep on growing this company with all
the managerial headaches that brings. Or I can sell it to a
buyer who wants to keep me on as head of R&D and keep
on making money, or I can sell it for less money to somebody
who will just take it over. I've been stuck in this for over a
month now, and I just can't decide."

"Well, my hunch is that you know what you want to do,
but that your own personal desires are running into what
other people want you to do. Any possibility of that being
what's making you sick?"

A thoughtful *philosopher* type with a lively *imagineer* intelligence, Paul took a few moments to take in what I had
said. Then he smiled, and the rest of the story tumbled out. It
seemed that his wife Susan, a very successful attorney, and
their two teenage children, Marissa and Michael, were argu-

ing fiercely for Paul to take the higher bid for the company and stick with it in order to maximize his investment (and their comfort). Paul's brother Dan was convinced that he should just sell and start something else that he, Dan, could help him with. His mother, meanwhile, felt that he should stay with what he had started and grow it to be as big as possible.

"Do you have any friends with whom you could discuss this, without their own agendas getting in the way?" I asked. It was then that Paul told me he was a Quaker, and that he had been wondering about convening a "Clearness Committee" to help him manage this conundrum. Of course! What a great solution. Paul left the session later with the following instructions: (1) set up a committee meeting as quickly as possible, (2) tape record it so that he could revisit his answers, and then (3) listen to the tape and bring to our next session some written comments about what he would hear in those tape notes. I also suggested that he pay careful attention to his dreams in the days before and after the session.

And so, the next Saturday morning Paul and five members of his Quaker Meeting went off to a cabin in the woods, and for three hours his Quaker friends just asked him questions, listening with patience and love to his answers, offering him no advice themselves, but calmly *leading him into himself* with questions like these:

- What do you like about the work you're doing now?
- How are things different now from when you started your company?
- If you didn't have to work at all, how would you spend your days?
- What are the things that matter most to you?
- What people are you trying to please?
- What do they want from you?
- What would you most like to do with your money?
- What do you think is God's purpose for you in this life?

In three hours, Paul was exhausted, but exhilarated, there in the honest quiet of the woods, warmed by the sun that seemed more and more insistent about touching him through the thicket of pines as it rose higher in the sky. Things had indeed become clearer for him. After lunch and warm embraces all round, the six friends went on their own separate ways, and Paul went home to begin the long process of making a plan that would be true to himself, and yet fair for the people in his life.

His list of solutions contained "something to offend everyone in the family," he joked later, but they were also carefully crafted to be consistent with his responsibilities both to his family and himself. He decided, ultimately, to sell the business to the lower bidder, to sign the noncompete clauses, and close that chapter of his puttering life. Ever the *imagineer,* he would, however, be free to putter at any of the million other things that floated through his brain on a daily basis. Even though the bid he took was lower than the one that would have kept him tied to the company, there was enough money to do the things he felt compelled to do. He set aside enough to pay for the children's college education, and he paid off his mortgage. The rest of his net proceeds he invested, so that he would have a smaller-than-usual but regular income. He also approached the small progressive private school where Mike and Marissa had once been students, and asked if he could try a "solving problems with your hands" course for the third through sixth graders there. As expected, the principal was jubilant.

Paul wasn't sure just what else he would do. But he knew that other opportunities to have his activities and his life passions be congruent would be coming along, and that he wanted to have the time to say yes. Susan and the children were unhappy at first, and his parents and siblings feared for his mental health. But Paul knew he was right. Susan was free to make whatever money she felt she needed, without comment or criticism from him. The children, meanwhile, were

assured a college education, and could work to earn whatever luxuries they felt they needed. He wished Susan were
free to travel with him to some of the special places in the
world that he wanted to visit, such as the rain forests, but
he knew that she needed to do what made sense to her. He
hoped she'd join him in due time.

Antoine de Saint-Exupéry knew what was happening with
Paul, when he counseled, "It is only with the heart that one
can see rightly, what is essential is invisible to the eye." Paul's
"Clearness Committee" helped him listen to his own heart,
and move through *reevaluation* to an open space, where he
would await instructions from within.

It Seemed Like a Good Idea
at the Time

*"The Graceful Exit . . . means leaving what's over
without denying its validity or its past importance
in our lives. It involves a sense of future, a belief
that every exit line is an entry, that we are moving
on rather than out."*

—Ellen Goodman

"I feel as if we're here talking about divorce," said Peg, a
striking, energetic 45-year-old, who had come with her business partner, Ninya, age 36, to talk about what to do with
their marketing business, Family Friends, Inc. Their niche was
helping small companies market family-friendly products.
Ninya, a Pakistani who had come to the U.S. as a student
and married her boyfriend upon graduation, added, "It's so
strange. Peg and I are so very alike, and yet so different at the
same time."

And indeed they were. The similarities? MBAs from the
same school and class, both happily married, mothers of two
boys apiece, and both marketing whizzes. They even looked
alike, with thick dark wavy hair and flashing eyes. But that's
where it stopped. "So tell me some more about the differences," I urged.

Ninya, the *philosopher,* started in. "Well, I feel badly about
this, but work just isn't as important to me now as it is to Peg.
My twins are much younger than her sons, and I feel that I
don't want to miss these early years. I also find that I really
like managing groups of people, which doesn't happen in a
business as small as ours. I never anticipated that. But Peg is
in her element when she's taking risks and trying new things.
And I really, really miss that predictable paycheck. So, my

fears and my sense of missing out on the things I really want to do each day have made me a crabby partner for these past two years. I know that's not fair to Peg, but I don't seem to be able to help it." A tear made its way to the corner of her eye, and then was joined by others.

"Wow, that's a clear dilemma," I responded. "Peg, is that the way you see things?"

"Pretty much," she said.

And so for the next hour we talked about what each one of them was looking for. It soon became clear that Peg's *free spirit/gambler* style was a great match for the demands of this new business, but that Ninya's style, complicated by the demands of her personal life, was not right now. As we talked, we began filling out an "Options Sorter" for each of them.

Here's what Peg and Ninya said was important to them:

PEG

1. Individual career identity
2. Excitement/challenge
3. Variety/change of pace
4. Meeting new people
5. Autonomy

NINYA

1. Time with family
2. Predictability—money
3. Predictability—time
4. Products she believes in
5. Managing others, more people

So how had these two ever decided to work together? In reality, when they first started out three years before, they had been a perfect pair. Good friends since business school, they had complementary skills and a hankering for an independent venture. So it had seemed natural to grab at the capital that a friend had made available and give it a try. But now, their circumstances had changed. Ninya had twins and wanted to be with them, and Peg's husband had been promoted into a very demanding job, leaving her with more time and wanting more, rather than less, independence.

It was time, therefore, for step seven, *reevaluation*. Our next task, after helping Peg and Ninya to draw up their lists, was to generate some possible options. And so they both went off to do their own research and networking to explore what might be possible. I met with each of them individually several times during the "exploring options" stage.

We came together again as a threesome when they both had their lists of possible options. Peg had come up with the following three possibilities:

- Keeping the business going on her own, gradually buying out Ninya
- Finding a new partner
- Taking a new job as VP for marketing in someone else's start-up

Ninya, meanwhile, had chosen only two:

- Getting her job back in her old company
- Taking a job with a new, smaller company

And so, we blended Peg's and Ninya's *wants* and *needs* with the *options* each one was considering to continue making the "Options Sorter." Then we estimated the degree to which each of the possible options (on a scale of 1 to 10) would give them what they were looking for. (You can try your own "Options Sorter" in Part Three.) Here's how Peg and Ninya's turned out:

PEG'S OPTIONS SORTER

Wants/needs	Option A (going solo)	Option B (new partner)	Option C (new job)
1. Individual identity	10	8	6
2. Excitement/challenge	9	8	6
3, Variety/change of pace	10	9	7
4. Meeting new people	8	9	9
5. Autonomy	10	8	6
TOTALS	47	42	34

Peg saw the scores and broke into a wide grin. "Yes," she said, giving a thumbs-up sign. "I'm ready to take it on myself."

Here's what Ninya's exercise yielded:

NINYA'S OPTIONS SORTER

Wants/needs	Option A (old job)	Option B (new job)
1. Time with family	9	7
2. Predictability—money	9	5
3. Predictability—time	9	7
4. Products she believes in	6	8
5. Managing others, more people	*10*	*8*
TOTALS	43	35

Ninya didn't have the immediately joyful reaction that Peg had had, but as she looked at the numbers for a few minutes, she saw the wisdom of the difference in her scores. There certainly would be more predictability in the old job, where she was well respected and valued—they really wanted her back, and she wouldn't have to prove herself while her energies were so taken up with two small boys. She smiled sheepishly, then asked, "But is it really OK for me to back out and leave Peg alone? And what would that say about me?"

Peg beat me to a response. "Of course it's okay. It just means that for now my overdrive energy is telling me to go faster, and your desire to be with the boys and lead a more balanced life for a little while is telling you to slow down. We're just in different gears now, and we'll probably be shifting again. I've been there, I know. There's no right or wrong now, just differences."

"Absolutely," I responded. "You are indeed similar in many ways, yet wired differently, so that's two layers. What we're seeing now is the addition of a third set of variables—your own quite different life stages. And so your decisions have to be revisited and reworked constantly in response to all three of those." Ninya was clearly relieved.

Peg and Ninya worked out a fair division of assets over the next year or so, and Peg took the business forward. Ninya, meanwhile, took back her old job and stayed there till the boys were in kindergarten; then she teamed up with three other people in a new small company, working as a much-needed combination marketing and operations director.

Peg and Ninya's dilemma and resolution demonstrate the wisdom of Ralph Waldo Emerson's admonition that "All of life is an experiment. The more experiments you make, the better." *Reevaluation,* you see, is not only a necessary last step to the free agency process, but also critical for every working person, whenever signs of a poor fit appear. Our lives have *movable* parts, and yet, alas, most of us behave as if they are *stationary,* leaving us no ability to take them apart and put them back together in designs that work better for us. How much less stress, depression, anxiety, and illness there would be if more of us took a wrench to our careers more often.

And What About Writing?

*"Your writing can take you to places where you'd
given up ever being again."*

—Anne Lamott

More than half of the clients beyond college age who come
to me to help them think about organizing their work life differently eventually end up talking about writing. Some arrive
saying right up front that they have decided to make writing
their primary life's work and need help figuring out how to
do it. Some talk about other forms of earning their keep, then
segue gently into hinting that perhaps they also have an itchy
writing hand. Still others think of writing primarily as a way
to know themselves, to keep company with themselves for at
least a portion of each day or week. Whichever way, writing
is a natural tool for step seven, *reevaluating and considering
more change*.

Feeling words slip out of you and onto paper or a computer screen is a way to mark where you are, where you've
been, and where you may be going. Even clients of mine
who have clearly "made it" amassing fortunes and/or fame
somehow *still find a need* for this most simple and essential
of activities. Whether they are "accomplished" yet or not, one
of the things we often do together is figure out just what writing means to them. I've talked with three different styles of
writers over the years:

1. *The careerist.* This person is ready for the considerable
   sacrifice involved in making writing her primary identity. Perhaps she's a writer-for-hire by day who does
   her own major creative projects on the side. Or maybe
   does her own writing whenever she can and keeps the
   bill collectors at bay by waitressing, caring for the el-

derly, or driving a bus part-time. Either way, she defines herself as a writer.

2. *The experimenter.* This person has a deep need to write but, for one or more reasons, is choosing to make this an auxiliary identity rather than his primary one. He's not sure how it will go, he's not at all certain he could (or would choose to) make writing all that he does. He wants to play with what the writing life feels like, in order to know how much of his daily existence he wants to give over to it. He has another role that he really likes and doesn't want to give up. Some people stay experimenters permanently, constantly shifting the degree of time and energy they are able to give to various projects. What defines them is their determination *not to have to choose* between writing and the other passions in their lives. Employers with nineteenth- and twentieth-century economic mentalities often don't understand this need, but the smart ones do—they know that some of their best talents keep themselves vital and productive on the job by having time to do their own thinking and writing away from work. In these work units, employees are encouraged to make a writing life for themselves, and to enrich their work for the organization simultaneously.

3. *The spiritualist.* This writer does it for love. She has probably bought all kinds of books about writing. She has carved out a space for her writing practice *because of the way it makes her feel.* Psychological research says very clearly that writing about your feelings (in fiction, poetry, journals, or in less structured ways) enhances your immune system and makes you less susceptible to illness. Writing is also very useful for figuring out what you're really thinking and feeling—it can be a kind of self-therapy. But probably even more important than that, for many people writing just feels good.

Writers are quintessential free agents, whether they profit from it financially or not. Just doing it gives them the *sense of personal control* so many free agents crave. What about you? If you picked out this story from the table of contents to read, it must be because you or somebody in your life has this "habit" that intrudes unabatedly into your life. Here's what you need to know about writing:

- It's scientifically proven to be good for you, physically, emotionally, and spiritually.
- You don't have to starve to do it.
- You don't have to do it all the time to get the benefit. The majority of writers, in fact, have other ways of supporting themselves.
- You don't need to earn any money at all to experience the ameliorative effects of having a writing practice.

But what does it mean to *have a practice*? Practice is used in many settings—it's about making music, learning to play a game or sport better, getting more proficient at doing almost anything. *Spiritually,* it's about making time *away from the fray of dailiness* to be with yourself, to dare to listen to your own frightened, joyful, and innocent voice, as well as the murmuring of something divine within you. When that forced quietness is combined with writing, the effects can be truly magical.

Many people write because they have to. Something inside them won't let them stop. If you suspect that might be true for you also, you don't have to know now whether you will write for money full-time, whether you'll write as an activity that's adjunct to some other definition of yourself, or whether you'll just do it because it makes you feel good and keeps you healthy. *Careerist? Experimenter? Spiritualist?* You don't really need to know. Just write, and the rest will take care of itself.

Daily Practice

*"Each morning we are born again. What we do
today is what matters most."*

—Jack Kornfield

In this quote from his *Buddha's Little Instruction Book,* Jack Kornfield could be speaking directly to free agents in step seven of the "working free" process. Who in the world needs the ongoing anchoring of a "daily practice" more than those folks who have traded their external rudders for internal ones? And when do you need it more than when you're *reevaluating*: testing the meaning of your work, deciding whether you should stay on the same track, fine-tune, or make significant changes?

Your daily practice may well be the most important thing you'll ever design. People who have taken training in techniques like transcendental meditation have one shared way of establishing their daily practice. Research shows that TM has many beneficial effects, not only for the meditators themselves, but for whole communities of people around them. Psychologists and physicians have made equally impressive discoveries about the efficacy of prayer. But these are not the only ways to journey inward. Others have devised different approaches to getting to a meditative state, according to their own preferences. What matters is that whatever compendium of activities or behaviors you choose *should make you feel peaceful and in touch with your real self.*

Over the years, I've talked with people who have developed an amazing array of daily "finding and grounding yourself" practices, such as:

- Meditation—silent or chanting
- Praying, at home, at work, out-of-doors, or in a church or temple

- Internal dialogues with real or imagined characters
- Walking or running outside in nature
- Long, hot baths, with music and/or candles
- Yoga
- Deep breathing
- Stretching or movement exercises
- Singing
- Playing a musical instrument
- Listening to classical or choral music
- Gardening
- Reading the Bible or other inspirational writings
- Dancing
- Sitting by the ocean or a lake or pond
- Walking on the beach
- Spending time with animals
- Writing
- Drawing or painting
- Working with clay
- Burning candles or incense

And there are so many more. The parts are indeed movable—you can combine them in any way that works for you. (See the "Daily Practice" exercise in Part Three.) Only *commitment, consistency, and time* really matter. You must choreograph a routine filled with whatever blend of activities settles your mind and takes you to a deeper, more knowing place. Take a month to experiment with *what mixture* of quiet and sound, or sitting still and moving about, will have the most centering and awakening effect for you.

Next, you have to give it time—somewhere between 20 and 60 minutes, once or twice a day—and do it every day. The ritual then becomes a cornerstone for you, helping you focus, concentrate, and zero in on what's important and what's not, amid the din of daily demands. If being surrounded by Mozart in their hospital incubators can get premature babies released from the hospital five days earlier than the preemies without it, then chances are *something meditative* could also have an ameliorative effect on your free agent mind and body. When you have established your daily practice and have learned to trust the inner knowing to which it leads you, you'll also find that it can help you make the critical choices in times of *reevaluation.*

Nora certainly found that to be true. She was wrestling with whether to take time out to attend a costly training program in herbal treatments to augment her work as an acupuncturist. She came to me because she was having a hard time deciding whether this would be the right move for her at this point in time. Her mentor was telling her that she should definitely do it, in order to stay competitive in the field of complementary health care. Her partner was telling her it wasn't worth the time or money now. And her friends were coming down commandingly on both sides of the debate. So she had come to get one more opinion.

"Why are you asking yet another person what to do when you have a way of asking yourself, the one true expert?" I asked her.

"What way is that?" she said, somewhat surprised.

"Didn't you tell me you meditate and do yoga each morning and evening?" I responded.

"Oh yes, I get all confused and out of sorts if I don't," she assured me.

. "So, what is your own well-practiced inner voice telling you now about this decision?" I queried.

Silence. And a stricken look of recognition. She had forgotten to ask.

"Well, I guess I figured that this was a practical matter," she stammered, "and so I needed to ask all the experts out there. Isn't that right?"

"You've done that now," I responded, "and you have more opinions than anybody ever needed. The only way to figure out which opinions come closest to your own inner knowing is to ask for internal guidance. Let me suggest a process to help you listen to yourself more attentively.

"Do your evening practice tonight and your morning practice tomorrow *as if you were going to the training.* Then write down how you felt—whether you felt lighter, and more confident, or heavier, as if you were going off to do something that isn't right for you now.

"And then the next evening and morning, do your practice *as if you were forgoing the training for now.* Again, write down how you felt—lighter, relieved—or concerned, as if you're missing out on something important. Then let's talk next week about what your own inner wisdom told you."

Somewhat perplexed but a little relieved, Nora went off to complete her assignments. When I saw her the next week, she seemed calm, but animated. "You were right," she said immediately. "I did those meditations from two completely different mindsets, and the answer was obvious. When I did the two sittings as if I were going to the advanced training, my whole body felt heavy and dutiful. My mentor was urging me to go and so I felt obligated, even though I knew I didn't want to.

"But the next day, the moment I was into the 'don't go now' mindset, I felt the weight lift from my shoulders. I knew that I needed to spend more time mastering the skills I already had, rather than adding on new ones right now. There was no longer a question about going or not going." I just smiled.

I must confess that it's not always that easy. Sometimes you do have to struggle with it a little more. But I promise that, once you've ferreted out all the relevant data, *nobody knows better than you what to do with it all!* Learning to be present with yourself, to be guided by your own feelings, body sensations, and hunches, is one of the most critical skills you'll need as a free agent. You must be self-aware and questioning through all the stages of working free, as we've said

repeatedly. But in the seventh step, the one where you decide whether to go or stay in your current venture, or how to
stay in a more in-depth way, or whether the person you've
become needs to do things differently now, *having a daily
practice is an essential life support system.* In this stage of
reevaluation, it's critical to believe and live by another Kornfield promise, that "if you take care of each moment, you will
take care of all time."

Part Three

HOW ABOUT SOME HELP?

"Working solo is not working alone."

—Terri Lonier

RESOURCES:

--→

Reading, Organizations, Links

BOOKS FOR POTENTIAL FREE AGENTS

Albion, Mark. *Making a Life, Making a Living: Reclaiming Your Purpose and Passion in Business and in Life.* Warner Books, 2000. Mark Albion has seen it all—from Harvard Business School professor to entrepreneur, and has concluded that the only way to real success is believing passionately in what you do. You'll find great role models for free agency in his 12 stories of people, including himself and his mother, who do indeed own their own lives.

Bridges, William. *Creating You & Co.: Learn to Think Like the CEO of Your Own Career.* Perseus, 1997. This book describes the new free agent economy and tells you how to make the most of it. Let Bridges help you figure out where you can market the skills you really want to keep on using.

Dinnocenzo, Debra. *101 Tips for Telecommuters.* Berrett-Koehler, 1999. If you're thinking of proposing a telecommuting role for yourself (yet another style of free agency), this wise little book will tell you how to ask your boss and then how to succeed at it.

Easton, Jaclyn. *Striking it Rich.Com: Profiles of 23 Incredibly Successful Websites You've Probably Never Heard Of.* McGraw Hill, 2000. These "real stories" will inspire you to follow your own passions and hunches to create a cyber-business that can work for you. It's a terrific mixture of practical and inspirational.

Edmunds, Gladys. *There's No Business Like Your Own Business: Six Practical and Holistic Steps.* Viking, 2000. Gladys tells it like it is. The book is like having a good talk with your grandmother, who just happens to know a lot about starting small service businesses.

Fisher, Roger. *Getting to Yes: Negotiating Agreements Without Giving In.* Penguin, 1991. In this crazy interconnected world, nothing is more important than being able to negotiate and maintain strong working relationships. This is a short book that feels like a lab exercise—don't miss it.

Gale Research Group. *Encyclopedia of Associations.* This annual directory, available in most reference libraries and career centers, lists associations by topics of interest. A great resource for budding social entrepreneurs.

Gallwey, W. Timothy. *The Inner Game of Work.* Random House, 2000. Whether you want to develop the courage to go out on your own, or need help getting people inside your organization to move into the twenty-first century and give you some space to be you, Gallwey's approaches to helping you and others change will be invaluable.

Godfrey, Joline. *Our Wildest Dream: Women Entrepreneurs Making Money, Having Fun, Doing Good.* HarperBusiness, 1993. This inspirational book is a great resource demonstrating the many ways and levels for doing your own thing.

————. *No More Frogs to Kiss: 99 Ways to Give Economic Power to Girls.* HarperBusiness, 1955. Here Godfrey "walks the talk" with suggestions for how parents, teachers, and youth workers can equip tomorrow's women to be ready to take care of themselves.

Goldberg, Alan. *Sports Slumpbusting: 10 Steps to Mental Toughness and Peak Performance.* Human Kinetics, 1998. So what does a sports psychologist know about being a successful free agent? Everything! Let internationally known performance psychologist and free agent Alan Goldberg show you how to take control of your own psyche to get the results you want with your business or free agency practice.

Goleman, Daniel. *Working with Emotional Intelligence.* Bantam Books, 1998. EQ (emotional awareness and interpersonal skills) is much more important to career success than IQ, says Goleman. In fact, many experts say that it accounts for up to 90 percent of workplace effectiveness. And nobody needs it more than free agents.

Horowitz, Shel. *Grassroots Marketing: Getting Noticed in a Noisy World.* Chelsea Green Publishing, 2000. Shel's "hands-on" guide to getting the word out if you're starting small and counting pennies is invaluable.

Kelly, Kevin. *New Rules for the New Economy: 10 Radical Strategies for a Connected World.* Viking, 1998. Don't even try to be an entrepreneur without understanding the ground rules of the new economy—both the opportunities and the land mines. This book is fun and eye-opening.

Knox, Deborah, and Sandy Butzel. *Life Work Transitions.com: Putting Your Spirit Online.* Butterworth-Heinemann, 2000. Because accurate self-assessment is such an essential part of the free agency process, and because being nimble with the internet is an absolute requirement for finding your way these days, Knox and Butzel's book may be a good way to move forward. It shows you how to peer into your own soul as well as where to turn online for the information and inspiration you need.

Lloyd, Carol. *Creating a Life Worth Living: A Practical Course in Career Design for Artists, Innovators and Others Aspiring to a Creative Life*. HarperPerennial, 1997. This book is full of gems for different ways to make art and make a living at the same time.

Lonier, Terri. *Working Solo: Smart Strategies for Growing Your Business*. Wiley, 1999, 2nd edition. Terri Lonier is the founder of the SOHO (small office/home office) influence group. She has a great web site (www.workingsolo.com) and several useful books. If you want to be working on your own, you can't afford not to have her practical advice.

————. *Working Solo Sourcebook*. Wiley 1995, 2nd edition. If you need a resource, chances are Terri's book can point you in the right direction. Books, tapes, web sites, associations— it's all here!

Lyon, Elizabeth. *Nonfiction Book Proposals Anybody Can Write: How to Get a Contract and an Advance Before Writing Your Book,* as well as *The Sell Your Novel Toolkit*. Blue Heron, 1995. You'd be shocked at how many people are secretly hankering to write. If you're one of them, these splendid books can show you how to make it a reality.

Matthias, Rebecca. *Mother Work: How a Young Mother Started a Business on a Shoestring and Built It into a Multi-Million Dollar Company*. Currency, 2000. You'll love the story of Rebecca and her husband Dan and how they built a company to produce executive maternity clothes. You'll be able to learn from their mistakes and emulate their successes.

Palmer, Parker J. *Let Your Life Speak: Listening for the Voice of Vocation*. Jossey-Bass, 2000. Palmer is an educator and word-smith whose frank descriptions of his own search for self, through job changes and depression, offer hope for anyone wanting to find more in life.

Peters, Tom. *Reinventing Work Series: The Brand You*. Knopf, 1999. Peters's tag line on this little book is "50 ways to transform yourself from an employee into a brand that shouts distinction, commitment, and passion." For folks who want to take a free agency mindset into their employment contracts, this is a great resource.

Petzinger, Thomas, Jr. *The New Frontiers: The Men and Women Who Are Transforming the Workplace and Marketplace*. Simon & Schuster, 1999. Petzinger's stories are about big fish and little fish in the new free agency pond. He combines his *Wall Street Journal* grasp of the economy with a natural storyteller's voice to make the challenges of today seem both real and manageable.

Seligman, Martin. *Learned Optimism*. Knopf, 1991. Nothing sinks a free agency ship faster than self-doubt and catastrophizing. If you're prone to either of these afflictions, get a copy of this classic book, take the self-assessment exercises, and follow the prescriptions religiously.

Thompson, John, and Catharine Henningsen. *The Portable Executive: Building Your Own Job Security—From Corporate Dependence to Self-Direction*. Simon and Schuster, 1995. In sharing the somber fact that there are currently more trained managers and executives than there are jobs for them, the authors exhort people in leadership positions to join the ranks of "portable" execs, yet another kind of free agent.

Toms, Justine and Michael. *True Work: The Sacred Dimensions of Earning a Living*. Bell Tower, 1998. Justine and Michael walk the talk of making spiritual passion the organizing principle of one's life work. Whether you want to strike out on your own or bring a more centered approach to working inside an organization, the Toms' sharing of their wisdom will be helpful.

Turner, Chris. *All Hat and No Cattle: Shaking up the System and Making a Difference at Work.* Perseus Books, 1999. The energy that radiates from this book by Chris Turner, "corporate outlaw," is what you'll need to borrow if you want to be a free agent inside your organization. She'll inspire you to have the courage to loosen things up—and make the business better in the process.

Yarnell, Mark and Renee Reid Yarnell. *Your First Year in Network Marketing.* Prime Publishing, 1998. Network marketing, the art of turning relationships into sales, is the "great equalizer" for people without a lot of formal education or business experience. If you're energetic and naturally good with people, this form of free agency may be just what you're looking for.

MAGAZINES AND JOURNALS

Fast Company Magazine. This is where the action is. The size and density can be daunting, but if you want to be sure you're on the cutting edge, either as a free agent inside an organization or out there on your own, you should consult this bible of innovation frequently. Call 1-800-688-1545.

Entrepreneur Magazine. The emphasis in this publication is often on franchises, but you'll find helpful trend information and the encouragement of lots of articles about people who are actually making free agency work for them. (www. entrepreneurmag.com)

Home Office Computing. This little magazine comes with terrific information on small office business solutions, as well as a surprising number of practical ideas for managing yourself as a free agent. Call 1-800-288-7812. (www.smalloffice.com)

Wired. Trends, opinions, and information about online and multimedia. Call 415-904-0660. (www.wired.com)

Inc: The Magazine for Growing Companies. Geared to somewhat larger businesses, but great for looking out ahead of the curve. Call 617-248-8000. *Inc.online* has different content, but provides access to print archives for research. (www.inc.com)

Harvard Business Review. The thrust of this weighty journal is corporate, but the trends are important to watch, even for little guys. Call 617-783-7410. (www.harvard.edu)

The Futurist. Stay way ahead by keeping your eye on the future. Published by World Future Society. Call 1-800-989-8274.

WEB SITES/ORGANIZATIONS

Web sites are a critical resource, but they change all the time. Here are a few "old faithfuls" to get you started. Since that's a relative term in cyberspace, let me include advance *mea culpas* for any of these sites that may have disappeared by the time you read this book.

Monster.com's "Talent Market." (talentmarket.monster.com) Read articles about free agency and post your services here. Get individual help on the free agent message board.

National Business Incubator Association. (www.nbia.org) Offers services and resources to potential free agents and links to member incubators.

Terri Lonier's Working Solo site. (www.workingsolo.com)

Small Business Administration. A reliable resource with regional and state offices. The SBA Answer Desk Help Line is 1-800-827-5722.

The Arthur M. Blank Center for Entrepreneurship at Babson College, Wellesley, MA. (www.babson.edu/entrep)

The Edward Lowe Foundation. (www.lowe.org) Tremendous resource for information and research.

SCORE (Service Corps of Retired Executives). (www. score. org)

American Association of Home-Based Businesses. (www. aahbb.org) Information, group purchasing, and networking for members.

Kauffman Center for Entrepreneurial Leadership, Kansas City, MO, 816-932-1000. (www.emkf.org) (www. entreworld.org)

Netscape's Small Business Center. (www.netscape.com/ smallbusiness)

National Museum of Women in the Arts. (www.nmwa.org)

Women in Business B2B Hub and Tools. (www. advancingwomen.com)

Working Today. (www.workingtoday.org) Nonprofit advocacy site. Includes new portable insurance program.

Women IT Professionals. (www.girlgeeks.com) Articles, message boards, and chat rooms to keep you connected to other women in technology.

Paul and Sarah Edwards' Self-Employment Site. (www. homeworks.com)

Aquent, Talent Agency for Creative, Tech and Web. (www. aquent.com)

eWork Exchange. (www.ework.com) Information about contract projects, training, and services.

The Riley Guide. (www.rileyguide.com) Terrific site for field, industry, organization, and association research.

Association of Management Consulting Firms. (www. amef.org) Assistance for managers and other professionals wanting to consider consulting.

Guru.com. (www.guru.com) Site to post services.

U.S. House of Representatives. (www.house.gov) Be sure they're passing free agent–friendly legislation.

National Speakers Association. (www.nsaspeaker.org) Nonprofit site to help you understand the business of speaking and connect with organizations.

International Franchise Association. (www.franchise.org)
Information, resources, and political advocacy.

Nolo Press. (www.nolo.com) Self-help legal information.

New Dimensions Broadcasting Network. (www.
newdimensions.org) For spiritually minded free agents,
the broadcasts, webcasts, seminars, and wisdom available through New Dimensions are invaluable. Justine
and Michael Toms have demonstrated an amazing ca-
pacity to engage with the most enlightened leaders,
teachers, and writers of our times.

Women in Technology International (WITI) (www.witi.
com) Information, resources, networking for free agents
and other women using technology.

For an updated list of relevant sites and other information
for free agents, potential free agents, and others mired in
career dilemmas, check my web site at www.barbara-
reinhold.com.

Where Are You?

---------→

Exercises to Get You Moving

MY OWN ALONE TIME EXERCISE

Directions: Take yourself to a quiet place. And on paper or into a tape recorder, record your answers to some of the following questions. Though this kind of "talking to yourself" might seem strange to you, it's necessary to tap into what you've hidden away beneath the busy-ness of your daily life. There's no need to reach any conclusions here—just practice letting your guard down and becoming more aware of what's inside you.

1. When is the last time I spent alone with myself? What feelings came up for me then? What do I hope (or fear) might come up for me now?

_____

_____

_____

_____

_____

_____

2. What could I imagine doing if I didn't have to go to work for a year? Could some of those things ever be part of a self-designed career for me?

_____

_____

_____

_____

_____

3. When I was a child, what things did I love? When I was a teenager? How could I get more of these things into my life now?

_____

_____

_____

_____

_____

4. What is my hurrying up about now? What's happening, either inside me or out there in the world, that I don't want to face?

_____

_____

_____

_____

_____

5. Whose approval am I trying to earn? Whom would I disappoint if I slowed down?

_____

_____

6. I'm so tired—what am I tired of?

_____

_____

_____

_____

7. What's missing for me? What would I like to add to my life now?

_____

_____

_____

_____

_____

8. What other thoughts and feelings have come up for me as a result of this exercise?

_____

_____

_____

_____

_____

Congratulations! You did it! Try this exercise again periodically, just to loosen up the "imagining" part of you.

MY OWN ASSUMPTIONS ANALYSIS

Directions: Here are some questions to help you identify some of the assumptions that might be influencing the choices you're currently making (or not making). Write out the answers to these questions in a notebook—or talk about them with somebody whose knowledge and judgment you trust. Then see what additional information you can find online or in print.

1. How likely is it that my job will exist in its present form in two years? In five years? What am I protecting by staying? Is it worth it?

2. On a scale of 1 to 10 (10 = things are terrific), how much am I really enjoying my work now? How long do I assume that it will last? What assumptions are keeping me there?

3. How likely is it that I'll be rewarded at my current job in a way I feel is appropriate for my hard work and extra effort?

4. How likely is it that my employer wants to keep me enough to give me more freedom about doing my work either part-time or in a flex-mode, if I take the time to show him/her that it would benefit the organization?

5. If I stay in my current job, who will be pleased or displeased with that decision?

6. If I were to strike out on my own, either full-time or with a part-time sidecar venture, who would be pleased and/or displeased with that decision? Why?

7. What is the likelihood that I could actually make a go of it if I dared to start a part-time or full-time venture of my own?

8. If I were independent, where could I find adequate benefits?

9. What is the likelihood that I'd enjoy work more if I were doing it my own way?

10. Would it be okay not to have a nine-to-five place to go to that I call "my work"? What other options are there? What might fit me?

11. What would it take to get started doing something I'd really enjoy doing? What resources would I need? Who could help me find them? Am I willing to ask?

Do you feel any more open now? This set of questions can be answered periodically. Assumptions are meant to be tested, alone and by talking to others—don't let yours sit there and influence you without questioning them!

MY OWN OPENERS VS. BLOCKERS GRID

Directions: Part of making things happen in the world is being open to new possibilities. Let the chart below show you how likely you are to let your own hesitations get in your way or keep you stuck in a situation that doesn't work for you. In each of the forced choices below, circle the number that seems most like your position between the two extremes. Think of the person who knows you best—and pretend he or she is looking over your shoulder as you answer. (Most of us tend to "fudge" on self-report exercises like these, but don't let yourself do that.) Then look at the pattern of your responses.

Openers							Blockers
Optimistic	1	2	3	4	5	6	Pessimistic
Confident	1	2	3	4	5	6	Self-doubting
Energetic	1	2	3	4	5	6	Lethargic
Risk-taking	1	2	3	4	5	6	Risk-aversive
Forthright	1	2	3	4	5	6	Timid
Trusting	1	2	3	4	5	6	Fearful
Accepting	1	2	3	4	5	6	Angry
Adaptable	1	2	3	4	5	6	Rigid

The qualities on the left are *openers* that make it easy to drop ideas that aren't working, to be confident about your abilities, and to move forward with new possibilities. The *blockers* on the right, on the other hand, are likely to keep you stuck in what's expected or easy. If you find a pattern of 4's, 5's, and 6's snaking down your page, then that lets you know you need to be talking to somebody—good friends, family members, your boss, or a counselor or coach—about how to get unblocked and on your way, wherever that may be!

MY OWN GHOSTBUSTERS EXERCISE

Directions: Wouldn't you like to clear out some of those irrational fears and negative expectations you've been carrying around—in order to make room for more optimism in your decision-making? This exercise will help you find out what unconscious "scripts" are influencing your ability to just let go and try new things. In writing or in conversations with a friend, family member, coach, or counselor, see where some of these questions lead you.

1. Name several people in your family or among your friends whom you really admire—what about them seems admirable to you?

_____

_____

_____

_____

2. Name some people in public life whom you really look up to. What's special about them?

_____

_____

_____

_____

3. What traits do you have in common with some of the people you admire?

_____

_____

_____

_____

4. Who are the "losers" who somehow bug you, in your family, at work, among your friends, or in public life? What about their behaviors, attitudes, or personal qualities do you dislike?

_____

_____

_____

_____

5. Here's a hard one—in your most honest moments, do you see any similarities between yourself and any of these people?

_____

_____

_____

_____

6. Are there any ways in which your unconscious fear of being like one or more of these people might be getting in your way now?

_____

_____

_____

_____

7. In your life, to whom have you looked for help in making major choices? What would that person (or persons) say to you now about the choices you're facing?

_____

_____

_____

8. What examples of risks being taken and not taken have you seen, particularly as a child or young person, in the lives of people close to you?

_____

_____

_____

_____

9. Who have been the "heroes" of your family? What qualities about them made people look up to them? What "stories" can you recall? Are those qualities relevant now? Do you still see them as heroes?

_____

_____

_____

_____

10. What examples of successful risk-taking have you seen in your family and extended family? What did those people do to succeed? (Be as concrete as you can.)

_____

_____

_____

_____

11. Now think of the failures you know about. What behaviors, attitudes, or skill deficits seem to you to account for the failures of people close to you who didn't achieve their goals? Again, be concrete. What do you see now that they might have done differently?

_____

_____

_____

_____

12. How are you different from the people in your family who have failed?

_____

_____

_____

_____

_____

13. Who in your life really believes in you? Make a list of those people here:

_____

_____

_____

_____

Go and call at least one of those people who really believes in you—it's time to surround yourself with people whose confidence in you can help you move beyond your stuck places! Remember to ask them to remind you of your talents and good qualities from time to time.

MY OWN SPACE-MAKER QUADRANT EXERCISE

Directions: Let the four quadrants below help you start thinking about getting some breathing room in your life. Imagine that your current job takes up no more than two spaces. If that's not true, don't let this stand in your way for now—you can deal with the "realities" later. But assuming that you had enough time, what other kinds of activities can you imagine adding in the other two quadrants?

Now look over your quadrants with someone you trust—and start strategizing about how you could change the design of your current work week or month to make room for some of the items in your "new" quadrants. If you can imagine it, you can do it!

MY OWN IMAGINATION BOOSTER

Directions: When you've been stuck in work that doesn't fit you for too long, are trying to dream up something to add some spice to your work life, or are trying to reenter the world of work after time away, many times your imagination seems to have a flat tire. If you're experiencing some of that now, use one or more of the following questions to get yourself on your way.

Suppose I gave you $1,000 to spend at your favorite bookstore this afternoon. What kinds of books would you buy? Why? What do your choices tell you about interests and values of yours that might be relevant to different career options for you in the future?

_____

_____

_____

_____

_____

_____

What are your favorite web sites? Are there any clues in those selections about the kinds of things you like to think about or be involved in? _____

_____

_____

_____

_____

_____

Think back over the past several months. When have you been jealous or envious of others? For what reasons? If you could have what they have, what would that do for you?

_____

_____

_____

_____

_____

Remember what you liked to do in grade school and junior high. What were you best at then? How did that feel? Can you imagine turning something related to those activities into a part-time or full-time activity now? _____

_____

_____

_____

_____

_____

_____

With whom would you most like to change places for a year? Why? What about that person's life is appealing to you?

_____

_____

_____

_____

What's the most fun you have in your life now? Is there anything related to those times or activities that could be developed into something you could get paid for?

_____

_____

_____

_____

_____

I've just given you a check for $100,000 to give away to one or more charities. To whom would you make your gift(s) and why? Do you see any clues there about what's important to you—and hence how you might put your passions to work in your own venture?

_____

_____

_____

_____

_____

If you were suddenly free (or if you are free) to find a new personal partner, what kind of person would you choose? Why? What qualities would you want that person to help bring into your life? What's the possibility that you could find some of those things _for yourself_ by changing how you do your work, or by adding something to it?

_____

_____

_____

_____

_____

Go out and start talking about some of these ideas, and get yourself to some of the print and online resources available to help you investigate some of what you've discovered about your own hidden passions.

MY OWN EQ CHECKLIST

Up to 90 percent of your career success comes from a compendium of skills, attitudes, and behaviors called "emotional intelligence." For free agents, the following five are particularly important.

On a scale of 1 to 10 (10 = "I have lots of this one"), estimate where you think you stand on each one.

EQ components for free agents   **Your Score—1 to 10**

Realistic self-appraisal/desire to improve/confidence
that you have the skills to meet your goals   _____

Adaptability/flexibility   _____

Optimism/generally positive expectations about life   _____

Self-control and follow-through   _____

Initiative and drive   _____

Next, show your "profile" to someone you trust—does that person agree with your self-analysis? If not, discuss the discrepancies.

Now you're ready to plan for how you'll come up to speed in these five EQ qualities. Perhaps your friend or a family member can help. You'll find good mentorship in the *Resources* section as well. Or you might want to think about finding a counselor or coach to guide you.

MY OWN FREE AGENT INFORMATION
INTERVIEW QUESTIONS

Identify people who are working full-time or in sidecar style as a free agent in fields or areas of interest to you. In some cases you won't be able to find a free agent per se, but could talk to someone who would have good ideas for creating a free agency venture in his or her field. Good sources for finding people to interview are your family, friends, neighbors, present or past colleagues, as well as alumni from your high school, college, or graduate school. Once you have their names, addresses, voice mail, and/or e-mail, contact the ones who sound most interesting and ask them if you could have 20 minutes to ask them questions about their work. Usually they'll say yes, particularly if you lead with the name of someone who sent you. Here are some questions you might want to ask:

1. If you are a full-time or part-time free agent, tell me how you decided to be one, and what it was like to get started.

2. What is it that you do exactly? How much time each week do you spend doing it? Are you involved in one primary venture, or in several?

3. What requisite skills and training did you need to get started? How did you get them?

4. If you're also an employee of an organization, how do you work out your divided loyalties? Does your "other boss" know about your free agent role?

5. If you're not a free agent, what opportunities for part-time or contract work do you see in your field? Is your employer open to contract relationships with free agents?

6. What kind of strategizing did you do to arrange your work to your own liking? What advice would you give to someone starting out to do that?

7. What about your field makes it hard and/or easy to become a free agent?

8. How old were you when you began working either full-time or part-time as a free agent? Does it matter how old you are?

9. How did you involve your family in the decision-making? Were there particular problems you had to work through?

10. What about resources? Where did you find business and legal advice?

11. How much money did you need, and where did you find it?

12. What are you doing about items such as health and disability insurance, as well as retirement?

13. Are there any books, organizations, or web sites (about your field or about the process of free agency) that you'd recommend as helpful?

14. Where do you go to find other free agents for help and companionship? Is there a kind of meeting that I might possibly attend with you sometime?

15. What are the best and worst things about being a free agent for you?

At the end of the interview, thank them for their time, and remember to follow up with a thank-you note within 24 hours. It's also courteous (and a good networking gesture) to let them know how you're doing from time to time and thank them again. *As a free agent, you can never know too many people!*

MY OWN VISION TEST

Here's one thing you can count on—nothing will come of your great idea until you're able to say clearly in one or two sentences *what your vision is,* and then outline on one page just how you intend to bring it to fruition. So why not practice right now? Make lots of copies of this page, which you'll date, so that you can keep your work in a folder. Then, as you fine-tune both the vision and the how-to outline, you'll be able to see your own progress.

Project name: _____

Today's date: _____

The Vision:

The How-To Outline:

MY OWN OPTIONS SORTER

Directions: Use this exercise to help you choose between or among options you're considering. It will help you measure how well each of your options matches the things/situations/experiences or results you're wanting in your life now. Step #1 is to brainstorm a list of five to fifteen items you want and list them down the left side of the page. Next, using the 0–10 scale (0 = doesn't do much, 10 = terrific result) for each of your needs, you can actually "score" how well each option would fit you. You can get an average for each option by dividing your numerical total by the number of needs/wants. It's important not to settle for options that don't really fit you—go for at least a 7 average before signing on for any of the options.

Current wants/needs	Option A	Option B	Option C

Total

Average Score

MY OWN RISK CONTINUUM EXERCISE

Where do you feel comfortable?

On the chart below, put an X on each of the four lines to show what your comfort level is about size, debt, risk, and income potential.

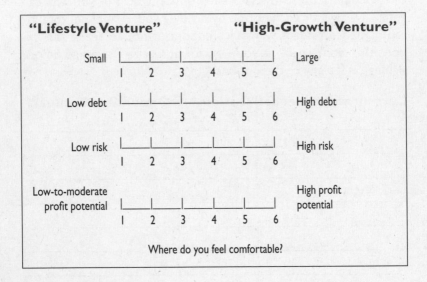

If you find yourself *mostly to the left,* then you'll probably be happier imagining a "lifestyle venture" rather than a "high-growth venture." If your scores are *mostly on the right,* then you're probably more wired for high-growth challenges. If you find yourself in the middle or split down the middle (some "lifestyle" preferences and some "high growth" expectations), then you'd better be finding a good coach or counselor to help you sort it out.

MY OWN GRADUAL TRANSITION GRID

Directions: On the chart below, play a game with yourself about *what might be possible* for you in testing out and adding products or services to your venture over the next five years. "Guesstimate" about what you'd do to generate income in both places, the number of hours you'd spend at your job and as a free agent, and how much money you might make in each venue. The emphasis here should be on *possibilities!*

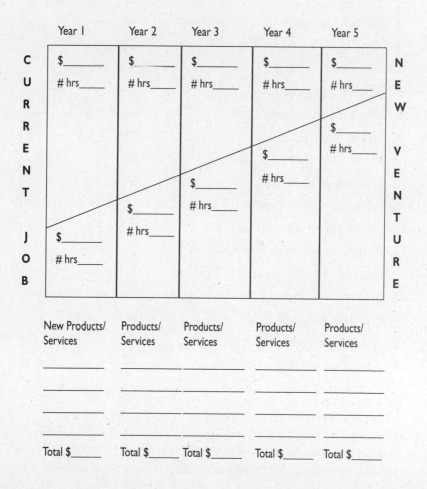

	Year 1	Year 2	Year 3	Year 4	Year 5	
C	$_____	$_____	$_____	$_____	$_____	**N**
U	# hrs____	# hrs____	# hrs____	# hrs____	# hrs____	**E**
R						**W**
R					$_____	
E					# hrs____	**V**
N				$_____		**E**
T			$_____	# hrs____		**N**
			# hrs____			**T**
J	$_____	$_____				**U**
O	# hrs____	# hrs____				**R**
B						**E**

New Products/ Services	Products/ Services	Products/ Services	Products/ Services	Products/ Services
_____	_____	_____	_____	_____
_____	_____	_____	_____	_____
_____	_____	_____	_____	_____
_____	_____	_____	_____	_____
Total $____	Total $____	Total $____	Total $____	Total $____

MY OWN RIGHT RHYTHM CHECK

If the work you're doing or thinking about doing doesn't give your body what it needs, then sooner or later it will let you know about it. Ask yourself the following questions about how well you're physically and temperamentally suited to your venture (or current job):

Requirement	Poor Fit	OK Fit	Great Fit
1. Number of hours of work per week	——	——	——
2. Time alone vs. with others	——	——	——
3. Time indoors vs. outdoors	——	——	——
4. Solo vs. team tasks	——	——	——
5. Work environment	——	——	——
6. Speed required	——	——	——
7. Variety and change of pace	——	——	——
8. Amount of downtime	——	——	——
9. Autonomy/time freedom	——	——	——
10. Office pace—slow or fast	——	——	——
11. Attention to detail vs. big picture	——	——	——
12. Degree of collaboration/competition	——	——	——
13. Starting and ending time each day	——	——	——
14. Holidays and vacations	——	——	——
15. Travel required	——	——	——
16. Flexibility allowed	——	——	——
17. Commuting time	——	——	——

So how's the fit? If you have more than 2 or 3 checks in the "poor fit" column, chances are you should do some hard thinking about whether you should be in that situation—and, if so, what accommodations you're going to negotiate or arrange for yourself.

MY OWN DREAM ANALYSIS EXERCISE

Dreams are a free agent's best friend, because they keep you aware of what's going on in your unconscious mind. When you're on your own, without a boss to keep you on track, you need to be able to count on your own internal course-correcting mechanisms. To stay aware of what you need to be noticing around you, use these dream analysis questions to understand the pictures and stories your unconscious mind is constantly sending your way.

1. Recall as much as you can about the dream.

_____

_____

_____

_____

_____

_____

2. Now that this dream has shown you that your unconscious is wanting you to think about or get help with a situation, do you have any idea what it might be? (Sometimes it will be obvious, other times not.) _____

_____

_____

_____

_____

3. What particular images or words grabbed your attention?

_____

_____

_____

_____

_____

4. What feelings do you remember having in the dream? What was the dominant feeling at the end of the dream?

_____

_____

_____

_____

_____

_____

5. What internal fears, doubts, or uncertainty did the vividness of the dream bring up for you? _____

_____

_____

_____

6. What external or practical questions or considerations are you wrestling with now in your work decisions that might be related to the feelings of the dream?

_____

_____

_____

_____

_____

_____

7. What good news is there for you in the dream?

_____

_____

_____

_____

_____

8. Now select several concerns that seem to be present in the dream and list them below. For each concern, decide if there is an action you should be taking, or whether this is a case of your "excessive worrier" at work. Should you instruct your anxieties to chill out for a while, or take some action now?

Concern   *Take corrective action or calm down?*

_____

_____

_____

_____

_____

_____

_____

_____

_____

_____

_____

_____

_____

_____

_____

Look back over all your answers to be sure you see the whole picture in the dream. If that's hard for you, you can ask someone to help you process it—and then you can help process that person's dreams in return. Dream analysis is a nifty tool for free agents.

MY OWN FILL-ME-UP TO GET WHERE I'M GOING EXERCISE

"Running on empty" is a condition that often strikes free agents, when they're trying to get started or have succeeded too quickly, and haven't made room in their lives for the extra demands. Here's an example you can use to help you figure out what's missing in the total picture of your life and, this document in hand, perhaps ask for the help you need. The chart below lists the things people are most often needing when they're on overload. For each item, list whether you feel you have enough of this resource now and, if not, where you might be able to find it.

Do you need more	Y/N	Where to get it?
• Time to do your work?		
• Physical help with work tasks?		
• Physical help with home tasks?		
• Relief from folks' demands?		
• Business or professional assistance?		
• Time for relaxation and sleep?		
• Time for exercise?		
• Emotional support?		
• Clear boundaries with your time?		
• Skill development		
• Technical assistance?		
• Networking to discuss problems?		
• Help with managing clutter?		
• Help managing your time?		
• Appreciation?		

Wherever you had *yes* answers, you know what to do—identify someone to help you find access to what you need and move beyond this burdened, stuck place!

MY OWN DAILY PRACTICE

Directions: Free agents benefit tremendously from designing for themselves a daily regimen of activities that center and balance them. The numbered list below can give you some samples from which to draw your own unique "daily practice."

POSSIBLE INGREDIENTS

1. Meditation—silent or chanting
2. Praying, at home, at work, out-of-doors, in a church or temple
3. Internal dialogues with real or imagined characters
4. Walking or running outside in nature
5. Long, hot baths, with music, candles
6. Yoga
7. Deep breathing
8. Stretching or movement exercises
9. Singing
10. Playing a musical instrument
11. Listening to classical or choral music
12. Gardening
13. Reading the Bible or other inspirational works
14. Dancing

My Daily/Weekly Plan

Which one?	How often?
_____	_____
_____	_____
_____	_____
_____	_____
_____	_____
_____	_____
_____	_____
_____	_____
_____	_____
_____	_____

15. Sitting by water—the ocean, a lake or pond, brook or river
16. Walking on the beach
17. Spending time with animals
18. Writing
19. Drawing or painting
20. Working with clay
21. Burning candles or incense

22. _____

23. _____

24. _____

25. _____

Etc.

MY OWN CLEARNESS COMMITTEE

Directions: The Quaker tradition of a *Clearness Committee* can be really useful for helping you to crawl inside your own thoughts and feelings, in order to know what's working beneath the surface in your life. If possible, ask several friends to go with you to a place that's removed from your daily experience, to help you consider a choice you're about to make. Have them ask you questions, some of the ones below and ones that come to them in the moment, to help you clarify what it is you really want.

1. What do you like about the work you're doing now? Is anything missing for you?
2. What are the things that matter most to you?
3. Tell us about the choices you're facing now—what does each one seem to offer you? What are the drawbacks associated with each one?
4. What are your happiest memories? What makes them happy for you?
5. Share with us some sad memories—what is that sadness about?
6. If money were no object, what would you most like to accomplish?
7. What makes you laugh out loud?
8. What's the most fun you've had this week?
9. When is the last time you cried? What was that about?
10. What regrets are hiding inside you? What would you like to do about them?
11. What would you like to do with your money?
12. What kinds of people do you like to be around? Why?
13. What do you think is God's purpose for you in this life?

There are no right or wrong answers here—only insights into who you really are. These questions can be useful in all the steps of the free agency process, from helping you to open up, to imagining, launching, fine-tuning, and reconsidering the whole thing.

GLOSSARY

Alternative officing: the practice of allowing people to work at home or in shared office space, in order to allow for more flexibility in schedules and to save on real estate and technical costs for employers.

ASP: "applications software provider," a company that assists free agents by automating the tasks generally associated with running a business, such as communication, billing, payroll, etc.

B2b: "business-to-business," a service or resource provided from one business to another. Many of the new internet start-ups fall in this category.

Contingency workers: people who work on short-term or project contracts, either within an organization or in their own space, as vendors of particular skills on an as-needed basis rather than as regular employees. These workers generally do not qualify for benefits from the organization. When contingency workers and regular employees work together on projects, as they often do, this is called a "blended workforce" situation.

Digital divide: refers to the diminution of opportunities available to students and workers who have not had access to technology and technical training. It will be increasingly difficult for people without technical skills and knowledge to earn a living wage in the information economy.

Employability: refers to organizations increasingly expecting their employees not only to pay attention to their current jobs, but also to take responsibility for keeping themselves skilled and marketable for the future. This means that workers can no longer count on their bosses telling them what training to take, but rather need to be assessing and improving their own skills all the time.

Flex-time: working on a flexible schedule rather than the "regular" hours of your workplace, generally to accommodate your own particular needs.

Franchise: a lower-risk way to start a small business, in that you don't have to dream up the idea yourself. You also have "best practices" counseling from corporate headquarters. Some people like the support, while others experience it as still having a boss.

Entrepreneur: one who starts and manages a business or practice, taking full economic responsibility for the endeavor.

Incubator: an organization that gives special help, in the form of training, coaching, resources, and/or venture capital to young businesses, usually in return for stock in the fledgling organization or a share of the profits.

Intrapreneur: one who starts up and manages a venture inside an organization owned or controlled by somebody else, taking on the challenge of making it successful, but without the full economic risk of entrepreneurism.

"Low-value" tasks: activities that have a low potential to make your business or practice more successful. Free agents must learn to recognize, and then delegate or ignore, tasks that don't have a high impact on the effectiveness of their endeavor, in order to make the most of their time.

Myers-Briggs Type Inventory: the most widely used personal style assessment tool in the world, helpful to individuals in figuring out which aspects of work and relationships will come most easily to them, and which will be more difficult. Available through many therapists, counseling centers, and career counselors.

New economy: an inexact term, used in different ways by different people, but largely assumed to mean an economy based on smaller, technical, or multimedia companies.

New free agent economy: a hybrid term, including, of course, the newer and more technical firms, but also the mushrooming number of sole proprietors, consultants, artisans, part-timers, and sidecar venturers, who are generally looking for more freedom and autonomy in their work.

Old economy: the bigger, sometimes more clumsy older brother to the new economy—encompassing "bricks and mortar" companies, as well as industries that were the mainstay of the U.S. economy 25 years ago, such as petroleum, steel, autos, and other heavy industrial products. The old economy assumption is that large companies can control obedient workers' lives, which is not necessarily the case anymore.

Outsourcing: a popular cost-cutting tool for employers, enabling them to "purchase" workers' services as they need them, rather than having employees on the regular payroll. Though widely criticized by labor unions and other groups as unfair to employees, this strategy also opens up opportunities for free agents to market their services to a wide range of employers.

Portability of benefits: the opposite of having your health insurance or pension plan linked to one employer. If workers had access to independent, portable insurance and retirement plans at an affordable rate, they would have less need to stay with employment that doesn't fit them. Though this hasn't happened yet, online purchasing groups in health, disability, and other insurances are a great step in that direction. In addition, the free agent advocacy group Working Today (www.workingtoday.org) has recently introduced a pilot portable insurance plan for free agents.

Redundancies: primarily in the lexicon of acquisitions and mergers, a euphemism for having one or more people in nearly duplicative roles as a result of merging two or more organizations. It's one of the reasons for the musical-chairs atmosphere in many organizations today, and generally results in jobs being lost.

Restructuring: can mean lots of things, everything from one company buying another and moving people around, to changing the structure of an organization in order to make way for a new leader or to fix an organizational problem. The bottom line is that people will usually be laid off.

Rosie the Riveter: a popular figure you may not know unless you're over 50 or a student of WWII history. The millions of women who went to work in factories in WWII were dubbed "Rosie," but found themselves summarily dismissed when the boys came home to reclaim their jobs. The big news is that, much to some men's chagrin, Rosie is here to stay this time, because most of the 65 percent of women who work like it that way.

Sidecar: a small business or practice which you begin in addition to your primary job. Some people have several sidecars going at once. Sometimes the goal is to grow the sidecar to a size where it becomes your primary income generator; and at other times it's something you intend to keep part-time as an outlet for your energies, interests, and talents.

Skill set: a group of skills you can "sell" to an organization, either as a regular employee or a contingency worker.

Social entrepreneur: a person who starts an organization, usually a nonprofit, not for the purpose of making a great deal of money, but rather to promote a valued cause or issue.

SOHO: a term used by Terri Lonier to describe the "small office/home office" group of contract workers.

Telecommuting: working from home or another location, for all or part of your workweek. Sometimes workers initiate the request to fit into their preferred work schedules, and sometimes companies initiate it as a cost-cutting measure.

Virtual organization: a group of people working "together" on projects without being in the same location—it exists in partnership and relationships rather than in a physical place and relies heavily on electronic communication.

White-collar robots: a term used to describe the effect of automation on how work is currently being done. Just as mechanical "blue collar robots" revolutionized manufacturing by working faster and cheaper than people, so are computers and the internet now providing "white collar" services that were once the province of office workers, bank tellers, "middle men," and mid-level supervisors. In both cases, the end result is the loss of traditional jobs.

BIBLIOGRAPHY

Albion, Mark. *Making a Life, Making a Living: Reclaiming Your Purpose and Passion in Business and in Life.* New York: Warner, 2000.

Antonovsky, Aaron. *Unraveling the Mystery of Health: How People Manage Stress and Stay Well.* San Francisco: Jossey-Bass, 1987.

Beck, Charlotte Joko. *Nothing Special: Living Zen.* San Francisco: HarperSanFrancisco, 1993.

Beck, Nuala. *Shifting Gears: Thriving in the New Economy.* Toronto: HarperPerennial, 1995.

Brehony, Kathleen. *Awakening at Midlife: Realizing Your Potential for Growth and Challenge.* New York: Riverhead, 1996.

Bridges, William. *JobShift: How to Prosper in a Workplace Without Jobs.* Reading, MA: Perseus, 1994.

———. *Creating You & Co.: Learn to Think Like the CEO of Your Own Career.* Reading, MA: Perseus, 1997.

Brody, Jane. "Personal Health: Paying the Price for Cheating on Sleep." *New York Times,* December 8, 1999.

Bromberger, Joyce T., and Karen A. Matthew. "A Longitudinal Study of the Effects of Pessimism, Trait Anxiety and Life Stress on Depressive Symptoms in Middle-Aged Women." *Psychology and Aging,* 1996. Vol. II, No. 2, pp. 207–213.

Bronte, Lydia. *The Longevity Factor: The New Reality of Long Careers and How It Can Lead to Richer Lives*. New York: Harper-Collins, 1993.

Business Week. "What's Behind Global Backlash?" April 24, 2000.

Business Wire. "Conference Brings Local Corporations Together to Discuss Employee Relations and Hiring Initiatives." May 15, 2000.

Butler, Timothy, and James Waldroop. "Job Sculpting: The Art of Retaining Your Best People." *Harvard Business Review,* September/October 1999, pp. 144–152.

Capelli, Peter. "Rethinking the Nature of Work: A Look at the Research Evidence." *Compensation and Benefits Review,* Vol. 29, No. 4, July/August 1997, p. 50.

Chart, Sewin, and Ann Huff Stevens. "Job Loss and Older Men." *Business and Management Practices, Monthly Labor Review,* Vol. 122, No. 6, June 1999, p. 40.

Cohen, Alan. *The Dragon Doesn't Live Here Anymore: Loving Fully, Living Freely*. New Jersey: Alan Cohen, 1981.

Conger, Jay. *Spirit at Work: Discovering the Spirituality in Leadership*. San Francisco: Jossey-Bass, 1994.

Cooper, Robert, and Ayman Sawaf. *Executive EQ: Emotional Intelligence in Leadership and Organizations*. New York: Grosset Putnam, 1996.

Crandall, N. Fredric, and Marc J. Wallace. *Work and Rewards in the Virtual Workplace: A "New Deal" for Organizations and Employees*. New York: Amacom, 1998.

Davidson, James Dale, and William Rees-Mogg. *The Sovereign Individual: Mastering the Transition to the Information Age*. New York: Touchstone, Simon & Schuster, 1999.

Dean, Bonnie St. John. *Succeeding Sane: Making Room for Joy in a Crazy World*. New York: Simon & Schuster, 1998.

DeLancy, Brian. "25 Best Business Opportunities for the New Millennium." *Home Business Journal,* September/October 1999, p. 12.

Dent, Harry S., Jr. *The Roaring 2000's: Building the Wealth and Lifestyle You Desire in the Greatest Boom in History*. New York: Simon & Schuster, 1998.

Dinnocenzo, Debra. *101 Tips for Telecommuters*. San Francisco: Berrett-Koehler, 1999.

Drucker, Peter. "The Future That Has Already Happened." *Harvard Business Review*, Vol. 75, No. 5, September/October 1997, p. 18.

Easton, Jaclyn. *Striking It Rich.Com: Profiles of 23 Incredibly Successful Websites You've Probably Never Heard Of*. New York: McGraw Hill, 2000.

Edmondson, Brad. "Hot Jobs." *Utne Reader,* January/February 1999, pp. 58–59.

Edmunds, Gladys. *There's No Business Like Your Own Business: Six Practical and Holistic Steps*. New York: Viking, 2000.

Edwards, Paul and Sarah. *Getting Business to Come to You,* 2nd ed. New York: Penguin Putnam, 1998.

Elgin, Duane. *Voluntary Simplicity: An Ecological Lifestyle That Promotes Personal and Social Renewal*. Toronto: Bantam, 1982.

Ferguson, Marilyn. *The Aquarian Conspiracy: Personal and Social Transformation*. Los Angeles: Jeremy P. Tarcher, 1980.

Fox, Matthew. *The Reinvention of Work: A New Vision of Livelihood for Our Time*. San Francisco: HarperCollins, 1994.

Gage, Amy. "Reinventing Work. It Will Be OK to Age in What Is Becoming a More Flexible Workplace." *San Diego Union Tribune,* February 28, 2000.

Gallwey, W. Timothy. *The Inner Game of Work*. New York: Random House, 2000.

Gerzon, Mark. *Coming Into Our Own: Understanding the Adult Metamorphosis*. New York: Delacorte, 1992.

Gibson, Rowan. *Rethinking the Future: Rethinking Business, Principles, Competition, Control and Complexity, Leadership, Markets and the World*. London: Nicholas Brealey, 1997.

Godfrey, Joline. *Our Wildest Dreams: Women Entrepreneurs Making Money, Having Fun, Doing Good*. New York: HarperBusiness, 1993.

————. *No More Frogs to Kiss: 99 Ways to Give Economic Power to Girls*. New York: HarperBusiness, 1995.

Godin, Seth. *Permission Marketing: Turning Strangers into Friends and Friends into Customers.* New York: Simon & Schuster, 1999.

Goldberg, Alan. *Sports Slumpbusting: 10 Steps to Mental Toughness and Peak Performance.* Champaign, IL: Human Kinetics, 1998.

Goleman, Daniel. *Working with Emotional Intelligence.* New York: Bantam, 1998.

Graham, John. "The Middle Man—Endangered Species." *Home Business Journal,* September 10, 1999, pp. 36–37.

Hakim, Cliff. *We Are All Self-Employed: The New Social Contract for Working' in a Changed World.* San Francisco: Berrett-Koehler, 1994.

Handy, Charles. *Gods of Management. The Changing Work of Organizations,* 2nd ed. New York: Oxford University Press, 1995.

———. *The Hungry Spirit. Beyond Capitalism: A Quest for Purpose in the Modern World.* New York: Broadway Books, 1998.

———. *Waiting for the Mountain to Move: Reflections on Work and Life.* San Francisco: Jossey-Bass, 1999.

Hanh, Thich Nhat. *Peace Is Every Step: The Path of Mindfulness in Everyday Life.* New York: Bantam, 1991.

Herman, Eric. "Interest on Credit Card Debt Adds Up to Big Trouble for Consumers." *Knight Ridder/Tribune Business News,* May 9, 2000.

Hirshberg, Jerry. *The Creative Priority: Driving Innovation in the Real World.* New York: HarperBusiness, 1998.

Hochschild, Arlie. *Time Bind: When Work Becomes Home and Home Becomes Work.* New York: Henry Holt, 1997.

Horowitz, Shel. *Grassroots Marketing: Getting Noticed in a Noisy World.* White River Junction, VT: Chelsea Green, 2000.

Justice, Blair. *Who Gets Sick: How Beliefs, Moods and Thoughts Affect Your Health.* Los Angeles: Jeremy P. Tarcher, 1987.

Kane, Mary. "Financial Know-How Still Rare." *New Orleans Times-Picayune,* May 12, 2000.

Kaufmann, Patrick J. "Franchising and the Choice of Self-Employment." *Journal of Business Venturing,* Vol. 14, No. 4., July 1999.

Kegan, Robert. *In Over Our Heads: The Mental Demands of Modern Life*. Cambridge: Harvard University Press, 1994.

Kelly, Kevin. *New Rules for the New Economy: 10 Radical Strategies for a Connected World*. New York: Viking, 1998.

Kimbrell, Andrew. "Breaking the Job Lock." *Utne Reader,* January-February 1999.

Kinder, George. *The Seven Stages of Money Maturity*. New York: Delacorte, 1999.

Kivirist, Lisa. *Kiss Off Corporate America: A Young Professional's Guide to Independence*. Kansas City: Andrews McNeel, 1998.

Knox, Deborah, and Sandra Butzel. *Life Work Transitions.com: Putting Your Spirit Online*. Boston: Butterworth-Heinemann, 2000.

Kornfield, Jack. *Buddha's Little Instruction Book*. New York: Bantam, 1994.

Langer, Ellen. *Mindfulness*. Reading, MA: Addison-Wesley, 1989.

Leifer, Ron, M.D. *The Happiness Project: Transforming the Three Poisons That Cause the Suffering We Inflict on Ourselves and Others*. Ithaca, N.Y.: Snow Lion, 1997.

Lerner, Betsy. *The Forest for the Trees: An Editor's Advice to Writers*. New York: Riverhead Books, 2000.

Lewis, Michael. *The New New Thing*. New York: W.W. Norton, 2000.

Lieber, Ron. "The Permatemps Contretemps." *Fast Company Magazine,* August, 2000.

Lloyd, Carol. *Creating a Life Worth Living: A Practical Course in Career Design for Artists, Innovators, and Others Aspiring to a Creative Life*. New York: HarperPerennial, 1997.

Lonier, Terri. *Working Solo: The Real Guide to Freedom and Financial Success With Your Own Business,* 2nd ed. New York: John Wiley, 1998.

———. *Working Solo Sourcebook,* 2nd ed. New York: John Wiley and Sons, 1998.

———. *Smart Strategies for Growing Your Business*. New York: John Wiley and Sons, 1999.

———. *SOHO Report: The New Summit on the Business Horizon*. SOHO, 2000.

Lyon, Elizabeth. *Nonfiction Book Proposals Anybody Can Write: How to Get a Contract and an Advance Before Writing Your Book.* Portland, OR: Blue Heron, 1995.

———. *The Sell Your Novel Toolkit.* Portland, OR: Blue Heron, 1997.

Matthias, Rebecca. *Mothers Work: How a Young Mother Started a Business on a Shoestring and Built It into a Multimillion Dollar Company.* New York: Currency, 2000.

Mattimore, Bryan W. *99% Inspiration: Tips, Tales and Techniques for Liberating Your Business Creativity.* New York: Amacom, 1994.

Miller, Annetta. "The Millennial Mind-set." *American Demographics,* Vol. 21, January 1999, p. 60.

Morris, James, Wayne Cascio, and Clifford Young. "Downsizing After All These Years: Questions and Answers About Who Did It, How Many Did It, and Who Benefited from It." *Organizational Dynamics,* Vol. 27, Number 3, Winter 1999, pp. 78–87.

Neef, Dale. *A Little Knowledge Is a Dangerous Thing: Understanding Our Global Knowledge Economy.* Boston: Butterworth-Heinemann, 1999.

Palmer, Parker J. *The Active Life: A Spirituality of Work, Creativity, and Caring.* San Francisco: Jossey-Bass, 1991.

———. *Let Your Life Speak: Listening for the Voice of Vocation.* San Francisco: Jossey-Bass, 2000.

Pearson, Carol S. "Working with Implicit Order." *The Inner Edge,* February/March 2000.

Peters, Tom. *Reinventing Work Series: The Brand You.* New York: Alfred A. Knopf, 1999.

Petzinger, Thomas, Jr. *The New Frontiers: The Men and Women Who Are Transforming the Workplace and Marketplace.* New York: Simon & Schuster, 1999.

Picot, Garnett. "Self-Employment in Canada and the U.S." *Canadian Business and Current Affairs, 1999* (Micromedia Limited), Vol. II, No. 3, Fall 1999, pp. 37–44.

Pink, Daniel H. "Free Agent Nation." *Fast Company Magazine,* December 1997.

Pogrebin, Letty Cottin. *Getting Over Getting Older: An Intimate Journey.* New York: Berkley, 1997.

Prokop, Lori. "Futurist Predicts: Returns on Home-Based Businesses Could Outpace the Stock Market." *Home Business Journal,* September 1, 1999, p. 53.

Reinhold, Barbara. *Toxic Work: How to Overcome Stress, Overload and Burnout, and Revitalize Your Career.* New York: Plume, 1997.

Rubin, Harriett. *Soloing: Realizing Your Life's Ambition.* New York: HarperBusiness, 1999.

Sawi, Beth. *Coming Up for Air: How to Build a Balanced Life in a Workaholic World.* New York: Hyperion, 2000.

Schor, Juliet. *The Overspent American: Upscaling, Downshifting and the New Consumer.* New York: Basic Books, 1998.

Schulz, Mona Lisa, M.D. *Awakening Intuition: Using Your Mind-Body Network for Insight and Healing.* New York: Harmony, 1998.

Seligman, Martin. *Learned Optimism.* New York: Alfred A. Knopf, 1991.

Sher, Gail. *One Continuous Mistake: Four Noble Truths for Writers.* New York: Penguin Arkana, 1999.

Sinetar, Marsha. *To Build the Life You Want, Create the Work You Love: The Spiritual Dimension of Entrepreneuring.* New York: St. Martin's, 1995.

Singhania, Lisa. "Kellogg workers who lost jobs to get government help." *AP State and Local Wire,* Grand Rapids, MI, April 12, 2000.

Spayde, Jon. "How to Think Outside the Cube." *Utne Reader,* January-February 1999, pp. 60–61.

Steiner, Andy. "A Path of One's Own: Five Who Transformed Their Dreams into Careers." *Utne Reader,* January-February 1999, pp. 51–57.

Stewart, Thomas. "Gray Flannel Suit? Moi?" *Fortune,* March 16, 1998, pp. 76–80.

Thompson, John A., and Catharine Henningsen. *The Portable Executive: Building Your Own Job Security—From Corporate*

Dependence to Self-Direction. New York: Simon & Schuster, 1997.

Tieger, Paul, and Barbara Barron-Tieger. *Do What You Are*. Boston: Little Brown, 1992.

Toms, Justine Willis, and Michael Toms. *True Work: The Sacred Dimension of Earning a Living*. New York: Bell Tower, 1998.

Toms, Michael, and Dee Hock. Interview, "The Chaordic Organization." *The Inner Edge*, Vol. III, No. 1, pp. 5–7.

Turner, Chris. *All Hat and No Cattle: Shaking Up the System and Making a Difference at Work*. Cambridge: Perseus, 1999.

Ueland, Brenda. *If You Want to Write: A Book about Art, Independence and Spirit*. St. Paul, MN: Graywolf 1987.

Vincola, Ann, and Caela Farren. "Good Career/Life Balance Makes for Better Workers." *HR Focus*, Vol. 76, No. 4, April 1999, p. 13.

Webber, Alan M. "Danger: Toxic Company." *Fast Company Magazine*, November 1998.

Weinstein, Matt. *Managing to Have Fun: How Fun at Work Can Motivate Your Employees, Inspire Your Co-Workers, Boost Your Bottom Line*. New York: Simon & Schuster, 1996.

Williams, Caitlin P. "The End of the Job as We Know It." *ASTD* (journal of the American Society for Training and Development), January 1, 1999.

Wylie, Mary Sykes. "Breaking Free." *Family Therapy Networker*. January/February 1998, pp. 25–33.

Young, Valerie. "You Don't Need a Job to Earn a Living." www.careerbuilder.com

ABOUT THE AUTHOR

Dr. Barbara Reinhold is into her fourth decade of free agency and having a terrific time! By day she directs the career development and executive development programs at Smith College in Northampton, Massachusetts. Her other enterprises include a private practice of counseling and coaching; consulting to corporations, small businesses, nonprofits, schools, colleges, and government groups; wrestling with career dilemmas online as the Career Coach for monster.com; giving speeches and seminars, including "Free to Succeed" workshops; and of course, writing. She lives with her family in western Massachusetts. For up-to-date information on her services and free career information and tips, visit her web site at www.barbara-reinhold.com.